Collins

English for Life

B1+ Intermediate

Writing

Kirsten Campbell-Howes
& Clare Dignall

Collins

HarperCollins Publishers
77-85 Fulham Palace Road
Hammersmith
London W6 8JB

First edition 2012

Reprint 10 9 8 7 6 5 4 3 2 1 0

© HarperCollins Publishers 2012

ISBN 978-0-00-746061-8

Collins® is a registered trademark
of HarperCollins Publishers Limited.

www.collinselt.com

A catalogue record for this book is available
from the British Library.

Typeset in India by Aptara

Printed by South China Printing Co.

About the authors

Kirsten Campbell-Howes has worked in the area of ELT for 15 years. She taught English in the UK and in Shanghai, China. Since then she has been writing and co-writing ELT books and digital products and has been working in this area for over ten years. Her writing includes a popular series for young learners, a series for young teens studying abroad and a General English series for adults.

Clare Dignall worked in publishing for many years, and, since childhood, has had a particular interest in the English Language: its history, its punctuation, its grammar, its sounds, and how all of these are evolving with us. Author of 'Can You Eat, Shoot and Leave?', the official workbook companion to Lynne Truss's international bestseller 'Eats, Shoots and Leaves', she has become a writer by accident rather than design. She lives in West Lothian with her husband, two children and more books than she has shelf space for.

CONTENTS

INTRODUCTION

Collins English for Life: Writing will help you to develop your writing skills in everyday life.

You can use *Writing*:
- as a self-study course
- as a supplementary material on a general English course.

Writing consists of 20 units, divided into the following four sections:
- Section 1 Writing socially
- Section 2 Writing to exchange information
- Section 3 Writing formally
- Section 4 Writing online for a reading public

Unit structure

For ease of use, each unit follows a similar structure. It is recommended that you follow the order of exercises when working through a unit. Each unit includes a selection from:
- A 'Before you start' section introducing the topic of the unit.
- Exercises under the heading 'Understanding' to check your comprehension.
- 'Looking more closely' exercises that ask you to look again at the texts that have been presented and notice new things.
- Language focus exercises that ask you to look in more depth at the language that has been presented.
- Exercises under the 'Writing clearly', 'Writing appropriately' and 'Get Writing' headings that ask you practise writing texts.

Other features
- There are boxed texts highlighted in green that present additional information relevant to the unit.
- There are also 'Useful Tips' boxes that provide useful information on the topic of the unit.

At the back of the book there are the following useful documents:
- Useful phrases for writing formal and informal emails, invitations, reviews, etc.
- Information on sentence structure, punctuation and short forms
- A checklist for proofreading your own writing
- A glossary providing definitions and example sentences for some of the more difficult words in the units.
- A comprehensive answer key which includes sample answers for all the questions in the book.

How to use this book

There are two ways to use this book:

1. Work through from units 1–20.

2. Choose from the Contents page the units that are most useful or interesting to you.

Language Level

Writing has been written to help learners at B1 level and above (Intermediate to Advanced).

Other titles

Also available in the **Collins English** series: **Speaking**, **Listening**, and **Reading**.

How to improve your writing skills

Many students think of writing as the hardest skill to master, but this doesn't have to be true. There are a number of simple steps you can take to improve your writing rapidly. The most important of these are:

1. Read as much as you can in a variety of media. Reading widely will improve your vocabulary and introduce you to new grammatical constructions.
2. Practise by writing as often as possible and experimenting with different styles and media. Don't be scared of writing. Think of it as a skill you will develop over time, just like speaking. Enjoy experimenting and welcome all feedback, even if it is negative at first.
3. Learn the rules of English grammar, sentence construction and punctuation. English is a large and complex language, but there are rules to guide you in how you use it. Don't be put off by these rules – once you have learned them, they will make life easier for you. Doing the exercises in this book is a very good start!

What is 'good' writing?

It is sometimes hard for people to agree on this question, especially when you are talking about literature such as novels and plays. But for general, everyday writing, there are some common characteristics that identify it as good. These include:

1. It is easy to understand.

This is not the same as 'boring' or 'simple'. Good writing can contain many unusual words and complex sentences but still be simple to read.

2. It is pleasurable to read.

As well as being easy to read, good writing should 'flow'. This is a hard concept to describe, but it is one we all understand instinctively. Think of a time when you have read something so quickly you can't believe you have finished it already – that is writing which 'flows'.

3. It is neither too long nor too short.

Sometimes this is about individual taste, but common sense can help. A 50-page list of instructions for how to turn on a television is far too long; a five-word summary of the causes of climate change is most probably too short!

4. It is communicative.

All good writing should communicate something to its readers, whether that is facts, opinion, feelings or inspiration!

1 EMAILS TO FRIENDS

BEFORE YOU START

Have you ever emailed a friend in English? Emails are a quick and easy way to write to anyone, wherever they are in the world. Because they are so adaptable, you will find that there are very few rules about what makes a 'good' email. However, there are a number of different approaches you can take when writing emails to a friend – practising these will help you improve your writing style.

Understanding

Read the email opposite. What two things does Nicole ask Katy to do?

1 …………..…………...……………

2 …………..…………...……………

Writing appropriately

Colloquial language is natural language that is used between friends in informal speech and writing.

Example *Yo, what's up!* (colloquial way to say 'Hello. How are you?')

1 **Read the email again. Underline five examples of colloquial language. What does each phrase mean?**

Example *How's it going?* = How are you?

2 **Read the sentences and phrases 1–5 below. Rewrite them using colloquial language.**

1 Hello.   ………………………….……………

2 How are you?   ………………………….……………

3 I don't understand.   ………………………….……………

4 Please tell me about what is happening.   ………………………….……………

5 I'm sad that I can't see you very often.   ………………………….……………

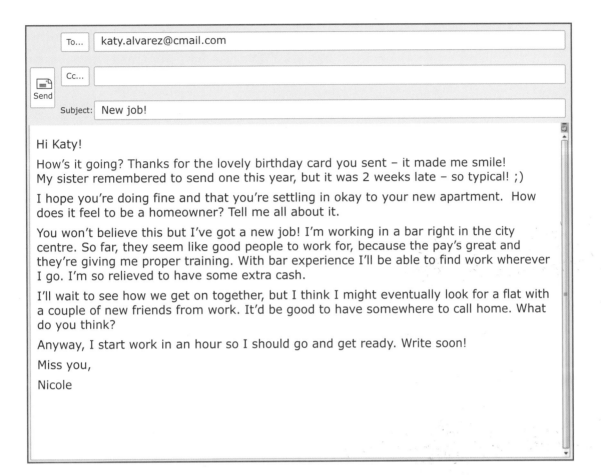

To... katy.alvarez@cmail.com

Cc...

Send

Subject: New job!

Hi Katy!

How's it going? Thanks for the lovely birthday card you sent – it made me smile! My sister remembered to send one this year, but it was 2 weeks late – so typical! ;)

I hope you're doing fine and that you're settling in okay to your new apartment. How does it feel to be a homeowner? Tell me all about it.

You won't believe this but I've got a new job! I'm working in a bar right in the city centre. So far, they seem like good people to work for, because the pay's great and they're giving me proper training. With bar experience I'll be able to find work wherever I go. I'm so relieved to have some extra cash.

I'll wait to see how we get on together, but I think I might eventually look for a flat with a couple of new friends from work. It'd be good to have somewhere to call home. What do you think?

Anyway, I start work in an hour so I should go and get ready. Write soon!

Miss you,

Nicole

Colloquial language

Colloquial language varies considerably from place to place. No one expects you to learn it all, but don't be afraid to ask the meaning if you see a phrase you don't understand. Here are a few examples:

USA/Canada: *Sure.* (= Certainly.)

Australia: *See you this arvo.* (= We'll meet this afternoon.)

Scotland: *Nae bother.* (= It's not a problem.)

Ireland: *Grand!* (= Great, Excellent)

USA/Canada: *Yeah, I reckon.* (= Yes, I agree, Yes, that's right.)

England (Yorkshire): *Eyup.* (= Hello.)

England (London): *Innit.* (= short for 'isn't it?', often used at the end of a statement)

Writing informally

Although emails to friends are generally informal, that doesn't mean they should all be written the same way. For example, you would write differently to a friend you have known since childhood and a friend you met two weeks ago. You shouldn't necessarily always write in the same way to the same friend, either. As an example, if your friend is unhappy and needs cheering up, you might write more seriously, and miss out your usual jokes.

3 **Match the opening sentences 1–4 to the purpose of the emails a–d.**

1 Hi Alek. This is James. We met at Maia's dinner party last week.

2 Jonas, Hi. I just wanted to write and say how sorry I was to hear about what happened.

3 Hello Misty. I thought I'd write and see how you are, and suggest a trip to the cinema.

4 Hi Jacopo. I know it's been ages, but I thought it was time to get in touch.

a an email to a possible new friend

b an email to a friend you haven't written to in a while

c an email to a friend who needs cheering up

d an email to a friend who has had bad news

Modal verbs

Modal verbs are auxiliary verbs that we use to show how likely something is to happen, as well as to express ability, permission and obligation. Modal verbs behave differently from regular verbs: they do not take an 's' in the third person, and we use 'not' to make them negative.

Language focus

Complete each sentence 1–5 with one of the modal verbs from the box.

1 I .... go now. I need to get ready for work.

2 We .... see Li Jiao next week. We've already bought the tickets.

3 I .... speak English, but I can't speak French.

4 Dee .... come to the party tonight, but she's not sure.

5 I .... help you with your homework if you really want, but I think you should do it yourself.

can		
		could
	might	
		will
should		

Get writing

1 **It can be hard to get the opening paragraph of an email right. Choose two of the following scenarios and write the opening paragraph and closing sentence of your email.**

1 You met a new friend several weeks ago and they mentioned that they were having a party this weekend. You would like an invitation to the party.

2 Your best friend from childhood is having a hard time at work. You want to cheer your friend up.

3 You have a very funny story to share with a good friend.

4 You borrowed your best friend's T-shirt and accidentally ripped it!

5 A friend you haven't spoken to for a while has moved into a flat with someone you like. You want to contact your friend again, but you would also like to visit and meet their housemate!

2 **Read the email from Nicole to Katy again. Write Katy's reply. Make sure you respond to the questions Nicole asked. Type your response using your preferred email software, and print out your work.**

USEFUL TIPS

- When you write a reply, include the original email that was sent to you. That way, even if your replies are very short, they will make sense to the reader.
- Even in informal emails, it is good practice to complete the 'Subject' field. Keep the Subject details short but informative, so your reader can tell immediately what you are writing about and whether you need a quick reply.
- Update your subject field if the email conversation moves away from its original topic.
- Remember, an email can't show your facial expression or tone of voice, so be very careful if you are trying to express a complicated or sensitive idea. If you aren't sure, ask yourself: 'How would I feel if someone wrote this to me?'.
- Unless your email is very urgent, you may have to wait a few days for a reply. Think carefully before you send another email to ask for a response. If it is very urgent, consider making a quick phone call instead.

2 TEXTING

Do you have a mobile phone or smartphone? Do you ever send texts? When it would be too difficult or time consuming to make a mobile phone call, you can use brief, personal messages or 'texts', also called SMS (Short Message Service), to write to people. A text can be a good way to make contact with someone when you do not need a quick reply; for example, if you are wishing them good luck for an interview or congratulating them on an achievement.

Understanding

Anita and Dominik have arranged to meet to see a film and have dinner, but things are not going according to plan. Read the SMS on Dominik's phone on the opposite page. What is the problem? How do they solve it?

Looking more closely

Find your phone and answer the following questions.

1   How many texts have you sent/received in the past week?

2   Are the texts you have sent and received different from emails? In what way?

3   Do you and your friends use any techniques to make your texts shorter to type? What are they?

Content words and function words

Sentences usually contain a mixture of content words and function words. Content words are often nouns, main verbs, adjectives and time phrases – they are the words that give us the meaning of a sentence.

Example   *There is a **party at** the **Students' Union tonight**. Are **you coming**?*

Function words are often articles, conjunctions, auxiliary verbs and prepositions. If you remove the function words from a sentence, your reader can usually still understand the meaning, which is why we often leave them out when texting. If you aren't sure whether a word is a function word or a content word, ask yourself: 'Would I still understand the sentence if this word was left out?'

Example   ***Party at Students' Union tonight. You coming?***

Language focus

1 **Both Dominik and Anita miss out words to make sentences shorter and quicker to type. Find the sentences where words are missing and write them out in full.**

Example *Train delayed 30mins. = My train has been delayed by 30 minutes.*

2 **Read the sentences 1–5 below. Put a line through the function words to turn them into texts. Do they still make sense?**

1 My car has broken down. I will be late for dinner.

2 What time is the meeting?

3 Can you buy some milk? I think we've run out.

4 I will be late for work. I'm sorry.

5 The restaurant is fully booked. What should we do?

3 **What do you think the following letters from texts refer to?**

1 u

2 b

3 LOL

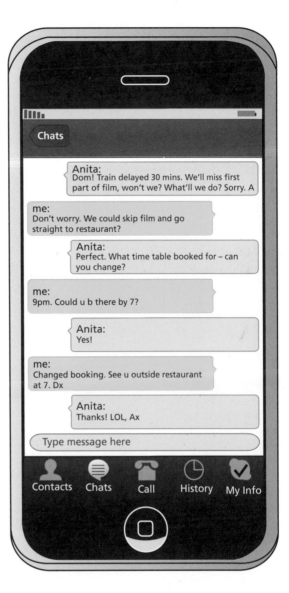

Chats

> **Anita:**
> Dom! Train delayed 30 mins. We'll miss first part of film, won't we? What'll we do? Sorry. A

> **me:**
> Don't worry. We could skip film and go straight to restaurant?

> **Anita:**
> Perfect. What time table booked for – can you change?

> **me:**
> 9pm. Could u b there by 7?

> **Anita:**
> Yes!

> **me:**
> Changed booking. See u outside restaurant at 7. Dx

> **Anita:**
> Thanks! LOL, Ax

> Type message here

Contacts Chats Call History My Info

Talking about texting

We use the word 'text' as both a noun and a verb:

Send me a text to let me know you got home ok.
Text me if you need anything.
I texted him but he didn't reply.

Note that in some countries, people replace the word 'text' with the acronym 'SMS':

SMS me if you need anything.
He sent her an SMS at three in the morning!

Sending texts is also called 'texting':

I don't like texting. I prefer to make phone calls.

Text speak

To save time and effort when texting, we often shorten words, using acronyms, abbreviations or keyboard characters to show what we mean. We call this 'text speak'. For example, only the first letter of each word in a phrase may be used instead of the full phrase:

- btw: by the way
- LOL: laughing out loud/lots of love
- omg: oh my gosh

Characters and numbers may be combined to create the sound of a word:

- b4: before
- m8: mate

Only the consonants of a word may be used instead of the whole word:

- msg: message
- pls: please

Repeated letters can be used in standard combinations:

- xoxo: hugs and kisses
- zzz: sleeping or bored

4 **Complete the following text conversation with text speak or shortened words from the box.**

Astrid: Fancy coffee tomorrow? 11 at Coco Matin?

Mathilde: Sorry – in bed with horrible cold. Maybe next week?

Astrid: Oh (1) .... poor thing – need anything?

Mathilde: No, all fine. Thanks (2) ....

Astrid: (3) ...., Pierre talking about
(4) .... again yesterday.

Mathilde: (5) .... ! What did he say?

Astrid: How (6) .... your date was and wants to
(7) .... again.

Mathilde: No! Really? Can u come round? We (8) ....
talk more.

Astrid: Course! C u in 15 mins, (9) .... ! xxx

Mathilde: Fab! Xoxo

OMG		u
	gr8	
		C u
	tho	
		LOL
BTW	cd.	

⑤ Change the sentences 1–3 to text speak.

1 See you tomorrow.

2 How are you?

3 I saw John yesterday. He told me a great story. It was so funny!

Get writing

① Write texts for the following situations 1–6.

1 Your friend has just been offered a great new job. Send your congratulations.

2 You can't find your house keys. Ask your flatmate for help.

3 You will be slightly late for work because you overslept. Let your boss know.

4 Your sister has had a baby girl. Tell your cousins the news and how the baby and her parents are.

5 Your friend has asked you to go out on Tuesday. You are busy on Tuesday, but not on Thursday. Suggest the new date.

6 You want to talk to your partner, but you aren't sure if he/she is free. Find out.

② Write replies to the following texts 1–3.

1 Locked out of flat! Am cold & freezing. Plz. help! : (

2 Hi! R u free? I've got a gr8. story 2 tell u! LOL!

3 Am gonna B l8 4 dinner! Sorry! Xxx

USEFUL TIPS

- Be careful not to use too much text speak. Texts are meant to be short, but they still need to be understandable. Ask yourself if the person you are texting will understand text speak.
- Sometimes, a phone call is actually quicker than a text. If you need to explain some complicated information that will take a long time to type into your phone, consider a phone call instead.
- Although texts can be delivered almost immediately, don't expect the other person to reply instantly. Many people like to turn off their phone during meetings or when they're with friends and family. Although texts may arrive silently, they can still interrupt people's activities.

3 INSTANT MESSAGING

BEFORE YOU START

How do you keep in touch with friends? In addition to texting on the move, you might use instant messaging (IM) on your computer or laptop. IM messages tend to be longer and more grammatically complete than texts because people often use a proper keyboard to type them (but they still might contain some shortened sentences, emoticons or text speak). Also, more than two people can message at the same time so the conversations can move fast and go anywhere!

Add   Topic   Profile   Call   Send File

Marika	Hey, you able to talk now?	(21:51:59)
Chris	Yes, but quite busy, so can't talk 4 long.	(21:52:48)
Marika	No probs. I've just got to tell you about what happened last night. ☺ LOL!	(21:52:59)
Marika	You're not going to believe what Karma did when she got to the party! She completely ignored all of us and started talking to this blond guy we didn't know. She couldn't take her eyes off him. We were wondering where Ben was and what he would say if he saw her!	(21:53:10)
Marika	And then Ben arrived and	(21:56:19)
Chris	Sorry to stop you, M, but I've gotta go to a meeting in a few mins. Just to change the subject, I wanted to ask if you'd heard from Baljit? He's been v. quiet recently.	(21:56:25)
Marika	Hold on a sec. Sbd. at the door…	(21:56:40)
Marika	Back! Sorry, you were asking abt. Baljit?	(22:01:31)
Chris is offline.		(22:01:50)

Language focus

1 **Marika and Chris are talking over IM. Read their conversation opposite. Note down the shortened words and symbols that they use. What do they mean?**

2 **Read the IM conversation again. Underline the phrases Chris and Marika use to (1) interrupt the conversation, (2) change the subject, (3) resume the conversation.**

Because we are often doing other things while talking over IM (especially if we are at work), interruptions are common. If someone is in the middle of typing a long message to you but you have to go (e.g. to answer the phone or go for lunch) you'll need to interrupt what they are typing to let them know. If you are planning to return to your computer quickly, you can let them know that you'll resume the conversation later.

3 **What is the purpose of the sentences 1–6 below? Write (I) for interrupting, (CS) for changing the subject, and (R) for resuming the conversation.**

1   Sorry, what were we talking about? ....

2   Can we talk about something else for a moment? ....

3   Just to change topic slightly... ....

4   Picking up where we left off... ....

5   Sorry to butt in here, but ... .

6   Can I just stop you for a second? ....

Language note

'Instant messaging' is also known as 'IM'. We talk about 'sending an instant message/ IM' and 'talking over IM', but we can also use 'instant message' as a verb:

Oh look, Dave is messaging you.

I'm going to IM you later.

If you want to talk about the act of instant messaging, you can use a sentence like:

Instant messaging is great – it's so easy to keep in touch with people back home.

Skype is a very popular instant messaging service – so popular that 'to Skype someone' has become a recognized verb for instant messaging. We also talk about 'having a Skype chat' or 'Skyping our friends'. Note that this can refer to an instant message conversation or an audio/video chat.

USEFUL TIPS

- When using IM, people might reply even faster than when texting, or leave the conversation for many minutes or more. As a result, you will need to react to interruptions, periods of silence and possible confusion, when talking over IM.
- When you are using IM, remember that your reader cannot hear your tone of voice or see your facial expression, so take extra care with what you write.
- Sometimes IM conversations can go on too long. If you want the conversation to end, say something like 'Gotta go now. Speak later. Bye!' There is no need to keep sending messages once you have both said goodbye.
- If you are too busy to respond to an IM (because you are in a meeting, for example), ignore it and respond later, saying for example, 'Sorry I couldn't reply earlier – I was in a meeting.' In many countries and cultures it is considered rude to respond to a text or IM when you are speaking with others. If you *must* reply, explain to the people around you, apologize, and keep your response short!

Writing appropriately

1 **Write IM messages for the following situations 1–3:**

1 You receive an IM from a friend that says: 'Are you there? I need to speak to you urgently!' You are sitting at your desk with your boss and another colleague, having an important discussion. However, you know your friend is having a difficult time and really needs to speak to you.

2 You are talking to your mother over IM when you hear a loud crashing sound and a scream coming from outside.

3 A friend is telling you a long story over IM. You are very hungry and want to go out for lunch.

Emoticons

Emoticons (also called 'smileys') can help your reader tell when you are joking ☺, or when you are expressing an emotion like disappointment ☹ or happiness ☺. Be careful not to use these too much though, as they can get annoying.

2 **What do these emoticons 1–5 mean?**

1 :D   2 <3   3 \o/   4 :0   5 </3

For more information on emoticons, see page 96.

3 **What emoticons do you and your friends use?**

Get writing

1 **Complete the conversation below with some suitable sentences. Keep them short – remember to miss out function words.**

Hey! Have 2 work late. Gonna be 30 mins late 4 dinner. Sorry! What shd. we do?

You: (1) ....

Great, thx! Where shd. I meet u?

You: (2) ....

2 **Complete the following instant message conversation. Use the prompts in square brackets to help you.**

Pete: Hi guys – can we talk? Stuck on tutorial questions we got today. No 4.

Shana: Yep, okay. Opening right now for a look, but only have 5 mins.

You: (1) .... [Tell your friends you will be with them shortly.]

Pete: Shana – you got to No 4 yet?

Shana: Hang on, let me just read it thru.

Shana: That's an unfair question! We haven't even covered that topic yet! How are we supposed to …

Pete: Hold on a sec, don't panic! I'm asking if that might be the stuff from the lecture we skipped last week.

You: (2) .... [Join the conversation again.]

Shana: We're looking at No 4 of those physics questions. Was that covered last week?

You: Think so. Got notes if you 2 slackers want them. Try turning up for lectures! ☺

Shana: Phew! Thx!

Pete: Could you email me notes tonight?

You: (3) .... [Answer Pete, then change the subject. Ask when the baseball will start tomorrow.]

Pete: 2pm, I think?

You: (4) .... [Apologize and explain that you have to leave the conversation.]

4 INVITATIONS AND RSVPs

If you are invited to attend a formal event like a wedding, you are likely to receive a traditional paper invitation, rather than an email. Writers take a lot of care over the wording and design of invitations; receiving an invitation is really the first part of the event! In such invitations, the language is often quite formal and old-fashioned. You might see phrases like 'request the pleasure of your company' instead of 'want you to come'. This language gives the invitation and the event more meaning and importance.

Understanding

Look at this example of a formal invitation. What event is this an invitation for?

> *Miss Fayah Kazmi & Mr Neil McGregor*
> *request the pleasure of your company at their marriage at*
> *Wells Manor House, Forrester Road, Alford, GR64 1SG*
> *on Saturday 7 July 2012 at 2pm and afterwards at*
> *Frensham Hall Hotel, Steading Place,*
> *Alford, GR62 2FL*
>
>
> *RSVP (with dietary requirements)*
> *by 1 May 2012*
> *11 Simnel Grove*
> *Haverton*
> *Surrey*
> *RH2 9PQ*

Looking more closely

Read the invitation again, then answer questions 1–4.

1 Where will Fayah and Neil get married? ....

2 Where will Fayah and Neil have a party after the wedding? ....

3 By which date must guests reply to the invitation? ....

4 When will Fayah and Neil get married? ....

Writing appropriately

1 **We use invitations for many different events. Match the events 1–6 with their definitions a–f.**

1	wedding	**a**	When two people get married.
2	engagement	**b**	An event to honour someone who has died.
3	graduation	**c**	When a person finishes their working career, usually in their 60s or 70s.
4	anniversary	**d**	When two people agree to get married.
5	retirement	**e**	A date on which people remember an important event from the past, e.g. their wedding.
6	memorial	**f**	When someone successfully completes their studies at school or University.

2 **As we have seen, invitations often contain quite old-fashioned, formal language. Using words from the box, fill the gaps in the common, formal invitation phrases 1–5.**

1 We request the .... of your company at …

2 You are .... invited to …

3 We would be .... if you could join us …

4 We ask you to be .... at …

5 We request the .... of your presence …

> cordially
>
> honour
>
> delighted
>
> pleasure
>
> present

3 **For more frequent, informal events like birthday parties, we use informal language in invitations. Fill the gaps 1–8 in this invitation using the words in the box.**

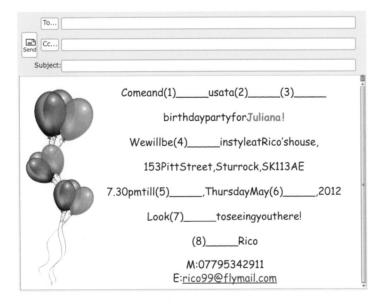

To...

Cc...

Send

Subject:

Comeand(1)_____usata(2)_____(3)_____

birthdaypartyforJuliana!

Wewillbe(4)_____instyleatRico'shouse,

153PittStreet,Sturrock,SK113AE

7.30pmtill(5)_____,ThursdayMay(6)_____,2012

Look(7)_____toseeingyouthere!

(8)_____Rico

M:07795342911
E:rico99@flymail.com

> forward
>
> late
>
> 17
>
> surprise
>
> celebrating
>
> 21st
>
> RSVP
>
> join

4 **Read through the RSVP examples 1–4 below. Which are formal, and which are informal?**

1

Gabriela and Manolo Navarro

 will be delighted to attend

the wedding of

Fayah Kazmi and Neil McGregor

on Saturday 7 July.

Vegetarian meals are requested.

2

Dear Eleni

We are very sad to say that we won't be able to come to your Graduation garden party on 9 June, because we are moving house that day. We would much rather be celebrating with you than unpacking boxes!

We both hope you have a fantastic day and that the sun shines for you. Well done on all your hard work. We'll be in touch soon after our house move.

Love and thanks,

Erik and Brigitte
xx

3

Dear Mr and Mrs L Cervantes,

We regret to say that we will be unable to attend your anniversary celebrations on 18 January 2012.

We send our congratulations and wish you every happiness for the future.

Jacinta and Anil Bhatara

4

Dear Ruxandra and Kristian,

Thanks for the lovely invite to your engagement party.

We'll definitely be there and can't wait to see you both!

Congratulations guys!

Lots of love,

Damien and Lily

USEFUL TIPS

- Many card shops stock printed RSVP cards for larger events like weddings. These will simply have a space for you to write your name(s). However, it is also perfectly acceptable to write your own RSVP. This gives you an opportunity to make your response more personal. Perhaps you might want to explain why you can't attend, or to describe how excited you are if you can attend.
- Always be careful that your RSVP goes to the right person, especially if, for example, parents are hosting the event.
- If you have received an informal invitation, you can reply informally too. You can use informal phrases like 'can't come' instead of the formal 'cannot attend'.
- Formal RSVPs often repeat the full names of the guests, and the time and date of the event. Informal ones will use first names and often omit the event details.
- Informal RSVPs tend to use the active voice 'We'd like the vegetarian meal option' rather than the formal passive voice 'The vegetarian option is requested'.
- Informal RSVPS are often longer and less precise, often including more personal or emotional words and phrases like 'can't wait' or 'lots of love'.

Get writing

1. Write an informal email response to Rico's invitation on page 17. Keep it short and simple.

2. Write a friendly, informal response to Fayah and Neil's invitation on page 16, using the information below to help you.

   - You are able to attend the wedding ceremony at 2pm.
   - You are unable to attend the evening reception at Frensham Hall.
   - You are happy that you have been invited to the wedding.
   - You are disappointed that you can't attend the party.
   - You know Fayah and Neil quite well, but you are not close friends.

3. You have been asked to write a formal postal invitation to a colleague's retirement party. Use the information below to help you.

   Name: Professor Alison Hylands

   Details: Retiring from Brockwell University's Chemistry Department after 25 years

   Party date: Thursday 9th August 2012 (7pm till late)

   Party venue: Rizzo's Italian Restaurant, 31 Byres Lane, Brockwell

   Requests: guests should describe any special dietary requirements (e.g. vegetarian food)

   RSVP: to Brian Barker, Brockwell University Chemistry Department by Thursday 2nd August.

5 THANK-YOU LETTERS

Thank-you letters (notes, or cards) are a polite way of saying 'thank you' to someone. It is sometimes difficult to know whether you should write a thank-you letter. For example, if a good friend gave you a small gift or bought you lunch on your birthday, a thank-you note is probably unnecessary. However, if you receive gifts at a formal event such as a wedding, anniversary or special birthday party, a thank-you letter is normally expected. In addition, if someone gives you a very valuable gift or does something very special for you, it is always polite to write and say thank you. If you really aren't sure, write one anyway – you are unlikely to offend anyone.

Understanding

Read this example of a typical thank-you letter. What did Katerina do for Mira? How do Lynne, Alec and Mira feel about it?

> 11 Broombank Avenue
> Holtville
> CA 33182
> 1 October 2012
>
> Dear Otto and Katerina,
>
> Thank you very, very much for the beautiful handmade quilt you sent for Mira's fifth birthday – all the way from Germany!
>
> She is absolutely delighted with it of course, because you have sewn all the characters from *The Gruffalo* into it. Otto, you must have remembered her telling you about the book when you visited in spring – what a good memory you have! Katerina, you are so talented, and you have put such a huge amount of time and care into making this quilt perfect for Mira.
>
> Yours is the kindest and most thoughtful gift Mira has ever received, and I know she will treasure it for many years to come. Who knows – maybe one day she will have children of her own who will love it too.
>
> With love and thanks to both of you,
>
> Lynne, Alec and Mira

Looking more closely

When someone does something nice for you, you usually express a reaction. Underline the parts of the letter opposite which express the following reactions.

gratitude   pleasure

surprise   admiration

Example   <u>Thank you very, very much ...</u> (gratitude)

Expressing reactions

When you want to express pleasure, gratitude, surprise or admiration for something someone has done for you, you can use a number of techniques.

Show the person you have understood how much they have done for you by writing about it:

...you have put such a huge amount of time and care into making this quilt perfect.

Use an adverb to make adjectives stronger and statements more intense:

***absolutely** delighted, **so** talented*

*Thank you **very, very** much.*

Use superlatives:

*Yours is the **kindest** and **most thoughtful** gift Mira has ever received.*

Praise the person for their efforts:

– what a good memory you have.

... making this quilt perfect.

Writing appropriately

Rewrite the following sentences to make them suitable for a thank-you letter.

1 Your gift was very kind. ....*Your gift was the kindest I have ever received.*.........

2 Thanks for organizing the party. ....

3 You cooked a nice dinner. ....

4 You worked hard organizing the party. It was fun. ....

5 The gift was pretty and I like it. ....

The past perfect tense

We use the **past perfect tense** to talk about an event that happened before another event in the past.

Examples   *I had wanted a new bicycle for ages!* (She wanted a bicycle for a long time and then someone gave her one.)

The party was a complete surprise. I hadn't guessed anything. (He didn't know his friends were planning a surprise party, and then he found out.)

Language focus

1 **We write thank-you letters to express our thanks for things that happened in the past. Read through the letter below and identify all the past tenses that are used.**

Example   *I wanted to write and thank you ...* (past simple)

> Dear Josie,
>
> I wanted to write and thank you so much for the fabulous party you organized for my 40th. I had no idea you had anything planned – it was such a surprise! Everything was perfect – it was great to see all the girls there looking wonderful. The food was amazing, and your decorations were spectacular! Most importantly, the birthday cake you made for me was the best I have ever tasted. (And I've tasted quite a few in my 40 years!) I've been telling everyone here what a fantastic night it was and showing them the photos. It just couldn't have been better – I felt so special. Thank you for all your hard work, secret planning, and for all the thought and care you put into the evening. It was the happiest night of my life. I'll remember it forever!
>
> With lots of love and thanks to my beautiful best friend,
>
> Andrea xxx

2 **Use the prompts 1–4 to write some sentences in the past perfect tense.**

Example   *(1st – didn't expect many people to be at the party) + (2nd – lots of people came to the party) = I hadn't expected so many people to be at the party!*

1 (1st – wanted to see the opera *Carmen* for a long time) + (2nd given tickets to *Carmen* as a gift)

2 (1st – didn't think anyone would remember my birthday) + (lots of people came to my surprise party)

3 (1st – always wanted to go to Russia) + (2nd – was taken on holiday to Russia by friends)

4 (1st – thought car couldn't be fixed) + (2nd – friend fixed car)

USEFUL TIPS

- The tone of your thank-you letter is more important than the format you send it in, but for a formal event or gift, it is best to respond by post rather than email.
- It is important to sound sincere. To do this, try to write naturally in the first person. For example: 'I really appreciate your kind gift.' sounds more sincere than 'Your kind gift is really appreciated.'
- It can be hard to get the balance right with a thank-you note: too many superlatives and your note may sound 'over the top' (=exaggerated), not enough praise and your note could sound 'lukewarm' (=not very interested) or ungrateful.

Writing appropriately

Read the following sentences 1–4 and decide if they are 'OTT' (over the top) or 'LW' (lukewarm). Rewrite them to make them more appropriate.

1 Your gift of a new electric kettle was simply wonderful – the best gift we received at our wedding.

2 Thanks for organizing my leaving party. I enjoyed it.

3 It was so very, very lovely of you to buy me lunch last week. It was the nicest thing anyone has ever done for me.

4 Thank you for looking after the house for two weeks while we were on holiday. The house looked quite tidy when we got back. We are grateful.

Get writing

1 **Write 2–3 sentences from a thank-you letter expressing a reaction to the following situations:**

1 A friend bought you a very nice gift for your birthday.

2 Your brother arranged a surprise birthday party for you and all your friends came along.

3 Your uncle fixed your car for free after it broke down.

4 Your colleagues bought you a lovely gift for your surprise leaving party.

2 **Now choose one of the letters from Exercise 1 above and write it in full. Remember to express your reactions clearly and to use a variety of past tenses.**

6 POSTCARDS

Postcards are a way of sending a short, informal message to friends or family. They usually have a photograph of your location on one side, with space on the back for an address and some brief news. Postcards should not be used for writing about private or important information or urgent matters. The space on them is limited, so we often shorten sentences and miss out words, sending someone a 'snapshot' of our time away, as well as something personal and fun for them to keep.

Understanding

Read the postcard below. Label the postcard with the terms in the box.

name and address	stamp	message text	greeting	closing message	signature

Hi Dani!
Hello from foggy San Francisco!
Arrived safely. Hotel is gorgeous, people are lovely. Weather is chilly, but who cares? We're enjoying every minute. Have already walked Golden Gate Bridge, eaten lobster and sour dough on Fisherman's Wharf and visited Alcatraz – scary! Watched the most amazing sunset last night – wish you could have seen it. Going to have a cable car ride tomorrow morning, if time. On Monday we're picking up the hire car and we'll probably drive on to Monterey first – we want to see Cannery Row!
Wish you were here!
              Marco and Christa

Place
Stamp
Here

Miss Dani Peters

23a Foghorn Lane, Newhaven

Edinburgh, EH37 4JG

UK

Writing clearly

1 **Look at the examples 1–5 from Marco and Christa's postcard. Write out the shortened sentences in full.**

Example   Arrived safely. *We have arrived (in San Francisco) safely.*

1   Hotel is gorgeous, people are lovely. ....

2   Weather is chilly, but who cares? ....

3   Have already walked the Golden Gate Bridge...and visited Alcatraz – scary!
....

4   Going to have a cable car ride tomorrow morning, if time.
....

2 **Now turn the full-length sentences 1–4 into short, postcard-style sentences.**

1   The weather here in England has been terrible.

2   We have been having a brilliant holiday.

3   In the last couple of days we have visited Cairo and the Pyramids.

4   I wish you could have seen the giant squid at the aquarium. It was terrifying!

3 **Read sentences 1–7. Decide if they are greetings (G) or closing messages (C).**

1   Wish you were here! ....

2   See you soon. ....

3   Weather is amazing! ....

4   We finally made it to Spain! ....

5   Greetings from sunny Florida. ....

6   Hope everything is going well with you. ....

7   We're having the BEST time! ....

Looking more closely

Read the postcard again carefully. Put a tick next to the things Marco and Christa have already done. Put a cross next to the things they are planning to do soon.

1   Drive to Monterey. ....

2   Eat lobster. ....

3   Pick up the hire car. ....

4   Go on a cable car ride. ....

5   Arrive safely. ....

6   Walk the Golden Gate Bridge. ....

7   Visit Alcatraz. ....

8   See Cannery Row. ....

Using tenses in postcards

A common way to structure a postcard is to start by saying how your holiday is going.

> *(We are) having an amazing time!* (present continuous)
> *(The) hotel is gorgeous!* (present simple)

The next step is to say what you have been doing since you arrived on holiday.

> *(We) visited the Taj Mahal and ate delicious curry.* (past simple)
> *We've already visited Niagara Falls.* (present perfect)
> *The kids have been learning to surf.* (present perfect continuous)

The last step is to finish by mentioning your plans for the next couple of days.

> *(We're) going to see the Terracotta Warriors tomorrow.* (future with 'going to')
> *We'll be flying home in three days.* (future continuous with 'will')

Language focus

Use the prompts 1–4 to write postcard-style sentences.

Example
(yesterday) + (lovely restaurant) + (fun) *Ate in a lovely restaurant yesterday – had so much fun!*

1 (every day) + (learn to SCUBA dive) + (challenging) ....

2 (first 3 days) + (have terrible jet lag) + (better now) ....

3 (two days ago) + (visit Eiffel Tower) + (beautiful) ....

4 (tomorrow) + (visit art gallery) + (exciting) ....

USEFUL TIPS

- Make sure you write your message on the left of the postcard and the address on the right.
- Don't forget to leave room for the stamp on the top right corner!
- Don't write anything in a postcard that needs a reply. An email will get a faster response!
- It would be unusual to put bad news in a postcard – save this for an email or phone call.
- Because space is so limited, it is acceptable to use shortened words and sentences.
- If your postcard doesn't have a picture or a name to show where you are, then you should say where you are in your message.
- In a postcard, it is acceptable to write with more exclamation marks, adjectives and superlatives than you would normally use.

Get writing

1 **Imagine you are on holiday in Australia. Take some notes on the following questions to prepare for writing a postcard.**

- How was your flight?
- Is your hotel nice?
- What's the weather like?
- Can you describe the people you've met?
- What food have you eaten?
- Which activities have you tried?
- What do you plan to do next?

2 **Read the words in the box. Circle the ones you want to use in your postcard.**

Sydney Opera House	amazing	concert	taxi	surfing
restaurant	beach nightlife		fun	relaxing
exciting	luxurious	scary	Great Barrier Reef	
hot	beautiful	Ayers Rock	barbeque	

3 **Fill in the postcard template with your message from Australia.**

Place
Stamp
Here

_____

_____

_____

_____

WRITING NOTES

BEFORE YOU START

Notes are short, informative pieces of writing that guide or inform you or someone else. You might, for example, take notes at a lecture in order to record the important points of what is being said. You may equally give some notes to a friend who is looking after your house or your pet while you are on holiday. These notes would describe all the things that need to be done while you are away, and explain how to do them in a simple and helpful way. Notes can be used for many different purposes, but should always be short, clear and uncomplicated – no one wants to read a long, puzzling essay just to find out how to work your microwave!

Understanding

1 **Here are some notes about how to look after a cat. How has the writer made the notes easier to understand?**

Normal day: to do

* Don't let her out!
* Half can of cat food: 8am & 6.30pm.
* Make sure water bowl is always clean and full.
Empty unwanted food in the bin outside back door. Wash bowls in utility room.
Litter tray stays in utility room: change litter after last feed each day.

Where things are

Cat food/ treats are kept in cupboard to the left of dishwasher. (Okay to give her 1 treat a day.)
Clean food bowls are kept   "   "   "
Litter tray/fresh cat litter kept in utility room.

Problems

NB in emergency, phone vet (Mr Curran) on 01963 458 339.
He will give directions etc. if you need to take her there.
Re. any expenses - I will repay you on return.

---

2 Read the notes again. Answer the questions 1–5.

1 What are the two most important things you should do?

2 What mustn't you do?

3 How often should you change the litter tray?

4 Where are the clean food bowls kept?

5 What should you do if you run out of cat food?

3 Read the notes below carefully. **What services are available at Villa Rosa? What responsibilities do guests have?**

Welcome to Villa Rosa – Some helpful reminders for your stay

The villa: Cleaner arrives at 10.45am Mon–Fri and will clean all rooms unless otherwise requested. All towels replaced daily. Laundry service is available – please speak to the cleaner to arrange.

Please ensure outside gate is locked each night and when you leave the property during the day. This is a no-smoking villa. Smoking permitted only in the garden and balcony areas.

Trams: Tram stop to Soller 200 metres from the villa. Turn left onto the main street as you leave the villa. Tram stop beside Pharmacy. Trams run every 30 minutes. Cost €5 return.

Shops: Nearest bakery and supermarket are only 5 minutes' walk. When you leave Villa Rosa, turn left onto main street then take first right at the park onto Plaja Repic. The bakery is straight ahead, (next to Hotel Mimosa) and opens at 6am. The supermarket is next door and opens 7am.

If you have any questions, phone Maria on 07798 652 312.

Looking more closely

Read the notes above again. Answer the following questions 1–4.

1 On which days will the cleaner *not* be cleaning the villa?

2 What do you do if you want to have your clothes washed?

3 Where can guests smoke on the property?

4 What is the name of the street where you can find the bakery?

USEFUL TIPS

Making notes for other people:

- All notes should be easy to understand, but you will need to take extra care with notes for other people. If you are writing your notes by hand, double check to make sure they are easy to read.
- Put the most important item at the top, or use stars (*) to show important points.
- Organize your notes into categories (e.g. cooking, cleaning, etc)
- Include your contact details in case there are questions you haven't thought of.
- Check and double-check what you have written. Would you understand these notes if you hadn't written them?

Symbols and abbreviations

Making notes for yourself is different from making notes for other people. When you are making notes for yourself you are often trying to write quickly to record the important points of what is being said before you forget them. It is only important that you understand the notes – no one else. This means that you can use techniques to write in a fast, meaningful way. Symbols and abbreviations are perfect for this. See how they are used in the example that follows.

Symbols and shorthand for making notes

&	and	"	repeat the text that you see above
+	plus	avg.	average
=	equals / is the same as	e.g.	for example
≠	does not equal / is different from / is not the same as	etc.	and all the rest
		i.e.	that is / in other words
>	is greater than / more than	NB	important
<	is less than	re.	concerning

What is Global Warming? Lecture notes 18/01/2012

Global warming = rising avg. temp of Earth's atmosphere & oceans.
Temp has risen > 0.7°C in < 100 yrs.
Many causes e.g. increased greenhouse gases from industrialisation, deforestation, population growth, fossil fuel burning etc.
NB Likely effects: extreme weather e.g. heatwaves, droughts, heavy rainfall, species extinction, changes in agric. yields.
Global dimming (i.e. increased reflection of incoming sunlight) counteracts the above but ≠ solution.
Re. global responses: see Kyoto Protocol.

Language focus

Another common note-writing technique is to abbreviate (shorten) common words by leaving out some of the letters, or substituting some of the letters for symbols.

What do these abbreviations mean?

1 w/ ....   5 ch ....   9 vs ....

2 w/o ....   6 p/pp ....   10 b/c ....

3 sbd ....   7 no/nos ....   11 min ....

4 sth ....   8 abt ....   12 max ....

something	because	page/pages	without	about
with	minimum	chapter	number/numbers	
maximum	versus	somebody		

Get writing

1 **Imagine you have some friends coming to stay in your house while you are on holiday. Think about these questions before doing Exercise 2:**

- Do you have anything that needs regular attention (e.g. plants or a pet)?
- Is there anything in the house that is difficult to use (e.g. water heater, door lock)?
- Does anyone else have a key to the flat (e.g. cleaner, neighbour)?
- Is there anything in the house your friends should/shouldn't use?
- Is there anything about the local area your friends should know?

2 **Now write out a complete set of notes for your friends. Remember to double-check your notes to make sure someone else can understand them.**

3 **Make some notes from the following voicemail messages, picking out the key information. Use symbols and abbreviations to save time.**

1 'This is a message for Katerina Frank. My name is Richard Hart, and I'm Head of the Linguistics Department at Keele University. We received your postgraduate application today. Please could you call me on 01463 435 291 between 9am and 5pm as soon as possible concerning your application. Your application has arrived without a research proposal and we need to know if there are perhaps some pages missing in error. Please do get in touch as soon as you can, because if we don't hear from you within the week, your application will, unfortunately, have to be rejected.'

2 'Hi Matt! I've found a flat for us I think! 63 Orchard Brae, Bromley. It has three bedrooms, and rent is at least £150 less a month than all the others we've looked at so far. It's five minutes' walk from the Tube station at the very most. Can you call the estate agent on 01395 456 989 to arrange a viewing? We have less than a week to view it, make a decision and pay a deposit. We'd better get moving. Remember to ask about parking!'

8 MAKING POLITE ENQUIRIES

BEFORE YOU START

When you are writing to someone you don't know, or writing to someone about a difficult topic, it can be helpful to use politer language than usual. If, for example, you have to make arrangements with a someone you've never met, polite language will help you get the right information and build a good relationship with your readers. If you need to write a difficult message to a good friend, careful language will avoid upsetting them and will hopefully get the result you want!

Language focus

1 **Read the email below. Underline the areas in the email where you see the following examples of polite language.**

1 A polite way to address a woman when you aren't sure if she is 'Miss' or 'Mrs'.
2 A polite compliment or praise.
3 A more polite way of saying 'I want to …' using a modal verb.
4 Polite phrases such as 'I hope that this is acceptable', 'please', etc.
5 Use of an 'if' clause to show that the writer understands that what he is asking for may not be possible.
6 A polite way of closing an email conversation.

From: hugo.koenig@avatar.com
Sent: 09 January 2012
To: m.valente@madeiravillas.com
Subject: Booking Enquiry September 2012

Dear Ms Valente,

After looking at your excellent website I am interested in renting your holiday villa, Cabana de Praia, during part of September. I would like to make a booking for six people altogether – two couples, and two children aged 1 and 2 (your website doesn't mention if you are happy for young children to stay – I hope that this is acceptable to you?).

As one of the adults in our group has difficulty with climbing stairs, I would like to enquire whether the villa has a downstairs bedroom or disabled facilities? In addition, would it be possible to arrange for a cleaner to clean the villa during our stay?

If you are happy for us to stay at the villa, please let me know which dates you have available in September. We are flexible about when we arrive. However, we would ideally like to stay for a minimum of ten days. An idea of total costs would be greatly appreciated.

I look forward to your reply.

Kind regards,

Hugo Koenig

Polite language

There are a number of techniques for making enquiries more polite.

- Using modal verbs such as 'would' or 'could' makes requests or enquiries 'gentler'.
  - *Tell me where the cinema is.* (impolite)
  - *Would you tell me where the cinema is?* (polite)

- Inserting polite words or phrases into enquiries makes them friendlier and more likely to get a response:
  - *A quick reply would be **greatly appreciated**.*
  - ***Please** could you let me have your response as soon as possible?*

- Using 'if' tells your reader that you are flexible and grateful for their co-operation. First and second conditional structures can be used to make polite requests.
  - *If you are happy with my suggestion, let's arrange a time to meet.* (first conditional)
  - *if you could give me the information I need, that would be great!* (second conditional)

- Adding a question mark at the end of a sentence, even when it is not an interrogative, can make a question sound softer:
  - *I would like to enquire whether the villa has a downstairs bedroom or disabled facilities?*
  - *I hope that this is acceptable with you?*

2 **Make these sentences 1–5 more polite with 'would' plus some of the words from the box.**

Example   *Tell me when your shop is open.*
         — Would you mind telling me when your shop is open?

1   Call me?
2   Give me your details.
3   What's your address?
4   I need a cleaner.
5   I don't know where the garage is.

> if
> possibly
> mind
> I wonder
> please
> could

3 **Complete these sentences 1–5 using the first or second conditional structure.**

Example   *If you could organize a cleaner, I would really appreciate it.*

1   If your hotel has some rooms available in March, ... to make a booking.
2   If the rooms have en suite bathrooms, that .... be great.
3   If you .... let me know whether breakfast is included, ... be most grateful.
4   If you .... happy with my idea, please let me know.
5   .... really appreciate it if you .... let me know whether your house is for sale?

4 **Read the following email and compare it with the email on page 32. Answer questions 1–3:**

1 Which email is more informal?

2 Which email uses more contracted words (e.g. 'I've')?

3 Which email uses full names and titles?

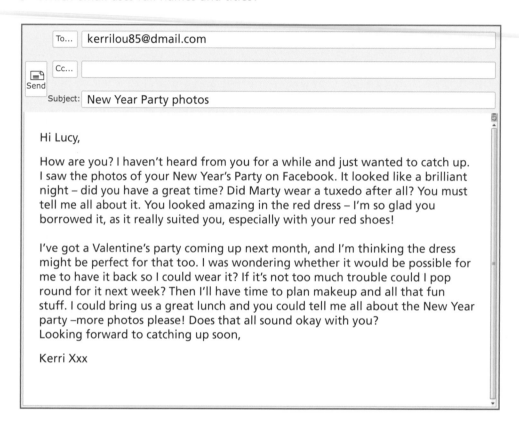

To... kerrilou85@dmail.com

Cc...

Send

Subject: New Year Party photos

Hi Lucy,

How are you? I haven't heard from you for a while and just wanted to catch up. I saw the photos of your New Year's Party on Facebook. It looked like a brilliant night – did you have a great time? Did Marty wear a tuxedo after all? You must tell me all about it. You looked amazing in the red dress – I'm so glad you borrowed it, as it really suited you, especially with your red shoes!

I've got a Valentine's party coming up next month, and I'm thinking the dress might be perfect for that too. I was wondering whether it would be possible for me to have it back so I could wear it? If it's not too much trouble could I pop round for it next week? Then I'll have time to plan makeup and all that fun stuff. I could bring us a great lunch and you could tell me all about the New Year party –more photos please! Does that all sound okay with you?
Looking forward to catching up soon,

Kerri Xxx

5 **Take a note of the polite phrases used in both emails in this unit. Add any other phrases you know to the list.**

Example   *... that would be greatly appreciated.*

....

....

....

....

....

Get writing

1 **Write a polite sentence for each enquiry 1–4.**

1 You want to find out where can you park your car at college.

2 You want to ask your boss for a day off next Monday.

3 You want to know whether there is a waiting list for tickets.

4 You would like to exchange an item of clothing that is too small.

2 **You are interested in taking an evening study course in computing at your local college. Write a polite enquiry to the college, asking for the information you need:**

- When is the class and how often?
- Are there still places available?
- Where is the class?
- How much does it cost and how do you pay for it?
- Does the college need any information from you before you can register for the course?

3 **Last year you lent your friend an expensive set of wine glasses for a party. They haven't mentioned the glasses since and you think they might have forgotten about them. You really need your glasses back as you are having a party soon. Write a polite and friendly letter to your friend to ask for the glasses back. Remember:**

- You are writing to a friend, so don't be too formal.
- Be polite, but firm.
- Stay friendly – your friend hasn't done anything wrong!

USEFUL TIPS

When you are making a polite enquiry ...

- Don't make demands, present options.
- If you are writing to someone you don't know, use formal language and tone. Don't use slang or abbreviations.
- If you are writing to a good friend, don't be too formal, as this can seem 'cold'.

9 GIVING INSTRUCTIONS

BEFORE YOU START

When you can't be there face to face to help someone do something unfamiliar, you can give them written instructions instead. You might, for example, give directions to your house when you send out a party invitation, or give some delivery instructions when you order groceries through a supermarket website. Instructions are everywhere, but they should all have one thing in common: clarity.

Understanding

Read the instructions in this party invitation. What kind of transport do you think Ashmi and Nikhil are taking to the party? What language tells you this?

From: roseanne.lau@blinks.com
Sent: 20 January 2012
To: dipendrafamily@cmail.com
Subject: Party time!!!

Dear Ashmi and Nikhil,

We're both really looking forward to seeing you on Saturday night. Here are directions to our place:

- Firstly, from High Street Colliers Wood, bear left onto Balham High Road.
- Secondly, turn left onto The Avenue, then take an immediate right onto the South Circular Road.
- After that, go straight on for one mile, pass by the hospital on your right, then take a left onto the A21 signposted Rushey Green.
- Follow this road for about half a mile, then at the roundabout take the first exit onto Loampit Vale.
- Next, turn left onto Breakspears Road before an immediate turn right onto Lloyd Villas.
- Finally, come down the hill to the end of the road. We are at number 2.
- Turn into our driveway slowly – it's a very tight corner but there is plenty of space to park once you are inside.

See you soon!

Roseanne and Han

Looking more closely

1 **Match the directions 1–8 to their meanings a–h.**

1	bear left	**a**	continue past; don't stop
2	take an immediate right	**b**	turn left
3	pass by	**c**	go straight / keep driving along this road
4	take a left	**d**	drive down the first road which you come to on the roundabout or motorway
5	follow this road	**e**	It is difficult to drive a car around this corner as there is not much space.
6	take the first exit	**f**	You will find us at house/building number 2.
7	We are at Number 2.	**g**	Take the next right turn, which is very close.
8	It's a very tight corner.	**h**	move your vehicle into the left lane of traffic

2 **Giving directions is very different depending on what form of transport your reader is taking. Read the following examples 1–8 and decide if they refer to travel by bus, train, car or on foot.**

1 Take the exit at Junction 16. ....

2 When you get to Darlington, change at Platform 2. ....

3 Turn left onto George Street and then climb the stairs outside number 56. ....

4 Go straight along Elm Row, turn left onto Peach Street and go past the post office. I'll meet you at the bench outside the bank. ....

5 After about 15 minutes, get off at the Plymouth Road stop. ....

6 After the turn off, bear left for 200 metres, then take the next exit. ....

7 Get off at Haslemere. Then cross over the bridge to Platform 1. Travel in the opposite direction for one stop, then get off at Frant. ....

8 Start at the Bowmere Road stop. Catch a Number 22 – there's one every 5 minutes. You need to get off again after about ten stops. It should take 20 minutes. ....

Language note

A good way to break up instructions is to use sequence adverbs. These words help to make it clear what order different steps need to happen in. Sequence adverbs include: *first/firstly, second/secondly, then, next, after that,* and *lastly/finally. Then, next* and *after that* mean roughly the same thing and can be used interchangeably.

Example

First, put the big key into the lowest keyhole in the door.

Then, turn it to the left.

Next, put the small key into the highest keyhole in the door and turn it to the right.

Finally, push hard and the door should open.

Language focus

Put the following instructions 1–6 in the correct order, using words from the box to fill each space. More than one answer may be correct.

1 ...., to secure your tent, use the tent pegs to secure the ropes around the tent.

2 ...., assemble the tent poles.

3 ...., unpack and separate the tent from the tent poles and tent pegs.

4 ...., clear the area where you want to put up the tent. Get rid of rocks, sticks, or other sharp objects.

5 ...., put the tent down on the clear area and unfold it so that the top is facing up.

6 ...., insert the tent poles into the sleeves around the edges of the tent. Keep going until all the main poles are connected to the tent.

lastly	first
	after that
second	
	finally
next	then

USEFUL TIPS

- Don't write an essay. Instructions need to be clear and easy to read. It's fine to use bullet points and short sentences.

- Instructions need to contain ALL the necessary information. Make sure you haven't left anything out.

- It may help to divide your instructions into sections or paragraphs, e.g. if you need to give instructions on how to get to a place and what to do once you get there, these two things should be kept separate.

- Remember to use sequence adverbs to put the steps of your instructions in a logical order.

- Remember that some things you find easy (like using your shower) might be complicated for someone who hasn't done it before. When you write instructions for something you find easy, try to remember what you struggled with the first time you followed these steps.

- Sometimes, a sketch or a diagram can be clearer than a set of written instructions. Consider including a sketch or a photo if it would make things easier for your reader.

- If you find that you have to give the same set of instructions over and over again, print them out on a piece of card to give to people. Alternatively, put them on a poster where people can read them easily.

Writing clearly

Simplify these instructions.

Example   *Take a potato and peel the skin off it carefully until there is no more skin on the potato.*

⇒ *Peel the potato carefully.*

Putting a fitted sheet on a mattress

Work out where the longer sides of the sheet are. Lay the sheet flat on top of the mattress with the longer sides next to the sides of the mattress and the shorter sides next to the top and bottom of the mattress. Pull one corner of the sheet around the corner of the mattress. Move to the corner of the mattress that is diagonally opposite the first corner and pull the sheet over this corner. Repeat the procedure just described with the other two corners.

Get writing

1 **Think about where you are right now. Write three sets of instructions for friends coming to visit you (1) by bus, (2) by car and (3) on foot. Answer these questions in your instructions.**

- Where is your friend coming from?
- Which parts of the journey might be confusing or complicated?
- Are there any problems or obstacles along the route (roadworks, for example)?
- How long is the journey likely to take?

2 **Your friend is coming to stay in your home while you are away. Pick one of the following options and write a set of instructions. If there is any vocabulary you need to know first, look it up in your Cobuild dictionary.**

- How to use the coffee machine / kitchen appliances.
- How to turn on the heating / air conditioner.
- How to lock and unlock the front door.
- What to do / Who to contact in an emergency.

3 **You are organising a surprise party for one of your friends. Write some instructions for your other friends.**

- Divide the instructions into two sections: 'Where to meet' and 'What to do'.
- Use sequence adverbs.
- Keep the instructions clear and simple.

10 WRITING TO CONFIRM ARRANGEMENTS

BEFORE YOU START

When you are making arrangements with someone, it can be very helpful to put them in writing. That way, your reader will have something to check if they forget the details. Often, to confirm an arrangement, you will find yourself repeating something that has been said before – when you were still in the 'organizing' stage. This is normal. A little repetition helps your reader remember the most important points.

Understanding

Read the email below. What arrangements is Hugo confirming with Ms Valente?

To...	m.valente@madeiravillas.com
Cc...	
Subject:	Booking Enquiry September 2012

Dear Ms Valente,

I am writing to confirm our stay at your holiday Villa, Cabana de Praia, from 9th to 19th September 2012.

As I mentioned previously, there will be four adults in our group, and two small children. Thanks for confirming that you are happy for the children to stay.

Our flight arrives at Funchal airport at 11.15am on 9th September. If we arrange to meet you at the villa at 12.30 to collect the keys, that should give us enough time to travel from the airport. (It shouldn't take too long to collect bags, and I am sure that the drive takes less than an hour.)

Thank you for arranging disabled facilities and a downstairs bedroom for us. It will make our stay much easier for everybody.

I am happy to pay the €150 deposit now. Would it be better for you if I phoned with my credit card details, or would you prefer a direct transfer to your bank? You can let me know what is easiest for you. You can also call me on 07789 345 112.

Best regards,

Hugo Koenig

Writing clearly

Writing to confirm arrangements can be useful if you later have a disagreement about something with the person you confirmed with. In the first example, Hugo writes: 'Thanks for confirming that you are happy for the children to stay'. This is a useful thing to say, as it gives Ms Valente another chance to consider whether she is happy for young children to stay at her villa. It also creates a written record in case she later decides she isn't happy about the situation. This type of confirmation is very useful in business arrangements, such as when you are buying something or hiring a service.

Some useful phrases for confirming arrangements include:

Can I just check/confirm that ...?

Could you confirm that ...?

Just to confirm, ... (+ details of what you think has been confirmed)?

As discussed/agreed, ...

... Is that correct?

1 **Use the phrases above to complete the following sentences 1–4.**

Example   *(Could you confirm that) the room will still be available tomorrow?*

1 ……….........……..................…., the whole order will cost £25.99, including postage?

2 You will meet us at the library at 6pm. ……….........……...….................

3 ……….........…..................…., these details are correct?

4 ……….........…..................…., you are happy to go ahead with the booking?

2 **Write a sentence asking for confirmation about the following things:**

1 ... that a hotel has rooms available this weekend.

2 ... that a payment will be made to your bank account this week.

3 ... that an order you placed will be ready for collection tomorrow.

Language note

We use the verb 'to confirm' to talk about making an agreement firm or to check that our understanding of an arrangement is correct.
I'm writing to confirm our offer of the position of General Manager to you.
Can you confirm in writing that the price of £12,000 is acceptable?

'Confirmation' is the noun form of 'confirm'. We can use it to talk about the act of confirming something, or to refer to a specific item (e.g. an email or contract) that proves an arrangement is confirmed.
Once we have confirmation of the price, I'll issue an invoice.
Geoff will send over the confirmation letter later today.

We can also use the adjective form 'confirmed' to refer to a firm agreement that has been made.
I've just called the bookings department and our flight details are confirmed.

Language focus

Hugo has written to his friends to confirm their holiday arrangements. How does he justify choosing the more expensive villa?

From: hugo.koenig@avatar.com
Sent: 13 January 2012
To: camilla.flockton@c.mail.com; peter.knowles@knowles-art.com
Cc: valerie.koenig@avatar.com
Subject: Holiday in Madeira: Booked!

Hi guys,

We are all set for Madeira! As you know we looked at two nice villas within our budget, and I've finally booked the Cabana de Praia, from 9 to 19th September.

I know this villa is a bit more expensive that the other one, but not only is the taxi drive there much shorter and cheaper, but the owner has put disabled access in the property to help us out. To be honest, she couldn't have been more helpful.

We fly at 7.30 am from Gatwick on the 9th, and will land at Funchal Airport at 11.15am. I've booked a taxi for 11.40 because it's a lot cheaper to pre-book, and that way we can guarantee a people carrier so we all can travel together. The owner will meet us at the villa at 12.30 with keys.

Let me know what you think of everything and if you have any questions.

Hugo.

USEFUL TIPS

When we confirm arrangements we've made, we sometimes need to explain or justify a decision. When we justify something, we present evidence as to why it was the correct thing to do. Look at these examples from Hugo's email:

… not only is the taxi drive there much shorter and cheaper, but …

Hugo compares one villa with another using comparatives (*more expensive, cheaper, shorter*).

He uses the phrase 'not only … but …' to show that he has two reasons for justifying his choice.

I've booked a taxi for 11.40 because it's a lot cheaper to pre-book, and that way we can guarantee a people carrier so we can all travel together.

Hugo uses 'because' to explain why he booked a taxi for 11.40.

'That way …' is a useful phrase for starting an explanation about why something is a good idea.

Get writing

1 **Write a sentence confirming arrangements in the following situations.**

1   You have bought a sofa from someone over the Internet and you want to confirm that they are happy to deliver it to you.

2   You are hiring a cleaner and you want them to come every Wednesday at 9am.

2 **Write some sentences justifying the following choices.**

1   You've bought a red sofa, not a black one. The red sofa was very comfortable. The black sofa was very small.

2   Buying a special ticket allows you to visit a castle and a museum. This is cheap. Buying two tickets is more expensive and it takes longer.

3 **You have arranged a birthday party for a group of your friends, including a trip to the cinema and a meal in a restaurant. Write an email confirming arrangements with the restaurant owner. Include the following information:**

- ten people will eat at the restaurant
- one person is a vegetarian, and one is allergic to nuts
- you want to eat at 9, and be finished by 10.30, as several people have a long journey to get home
- you are bringing a birthday cake to the restaurant as a special surprise

4 **Now write to your friends, confirming the evening's arrangements. Justify the following choices:**

- You chose a comedy film, rather than an action film. The comedy film was on early. You can get to the restaurant on time.
- You chose an Italian restaurant, rather than a Chinese. The Chinese restaurant was several miles away from the cinema.

11 WRITING A SUMMARY

When you write down the most important points from a piece of text, a lecture, or a sequence of events, you are producing a summary. A summary must be shorter than what is being summarized (usually a lot shorter). It should contain all the key points, but not all of the detail of what it summarizes. Summarizing skills are very helpful, whether in the workplace, when studying, or even in everyday life.

Understanding

Read part of the business report below on the left, and then the summary on the right. What are the differences?

PICKWICK ENTERPRISES

2011 was a difficult year for Pickwick Enterprises. Because of global economic downturn, Pickwick's total sales fell by 9% in comparison to the same length of time in 2010. Consequently, the company made the difficult decision to sell its least profitable division, Darwin Books, in summer 2011, which meant there were some unavoidable job losses.

However, 2012 will be a very different year. Pickwick Enterprises is delighted to announce new plans to restore staff morale and increase its profits. On 14 March 2012, the Company successfully bought the highly profitable, family-owned company Wonderland Toys, whose soft toys are famous for their quality, value and collectability. We are confident that this exciting development will improve the Company's financial profile, and reassure our loyal and valued work force that the future of Pickwick Enterprises looks very bright indeed.

> Although it had a tough year in 2011, Pickwick Enterprises is confident that 2012 will be much more successful. In 2011, the Company had some difficult times: there was a drop in sales, it had to sell Darwin Books, and some staff were made redundant. However, in 2012, the Company plans to improve the situation through its purchase of Wonderland Toys, which it hopes will grow profits and keep staff happy.

Thesis statements

A good summary will contain a thesis statement – a sentence that summarizes the main idea of what is being summarized. Look at the example from the report summary:

Although it had a tough year in 2011, Pickwick Enterprises is confident that 2012 will be much more successful.

This thesis statement copies the structure of the business report. The first clause (*Although it had a difficult year in 2011*) relates to the first paragraph of the report, which talks about the problems and difficulties of 2011. The second clause (*Pickwick Enterprises is confident...*) talks about the Company's hopes for a better 2012.

Of course, not all reports are two paragraphs long, but your thesis statements should contain the main idea or ideas of what you are summarizing. It might help to imagine that you are writing the headline for a newspaper story; what can you leave out and what must you keep in?

Writing clearly

1 **Read this article and write a thesis statement for it.**

Christmas spending spree expected

High street retailers say that they are looking forward to bumper Christmas profits this year. Contrary to what you might expect, research has shown that in periods of economic hardship, shoppers tend to buy more at Christmastime.

This behaviour is not too difficult to understand either; many of us have spent the year worrying about our jobs, sticking to a tight budget, given up our nights out, and even cancelled the family holiday to help make ends meet. It's no surprise then that we spend a bit more at Christmas to compensate for a hard year, make us feel secure, and to help see us through the bleakest months.

While there is no harm in indulging ourselves at Christmas for a bit of festive cheer, it's likely, however, that those who spend most will be the very people least able to afford it.

2 **Find a good quality newspaper. Cover up the headlines or ask a friend to cover them for you. Read the articles and then write thesis statements for them. Check your answers by comparing your thesis statements with the headlines.**

Plagiarism

A summary should be your own work, rather than a copy of what you are summarizing. If you copy sentences and phrasing from a source text when you write a summary, you are plagiarizing the author's work. Plagiarism is a form of stealing, and universities will usually impose strict penalties on students who are caught plagiarizing.

So how can you avoid plagiarizing when writing a summary? After all, a summary has to contain the same ideas as the source text.

The best way to do this is by paraphrasing the ideas in the source text. Paraphrasing involves changing the vocabulary and grammar of the source sentence so that it looks and sounds very different, but has the same or similar meaning.

Writing appropriately

1 Take another look at the summary of the business report on page 44.
Find paraphrases of sentences 1–4 below:

1 2011 was a difficult year for Pickwick Enterprises …

2 … total sales fell by 9% in comparison to the same length of time in 2010.

3 … there were some unavoidable job losses.

4 … will improve the Company's financial profile, and reassure our loyal and valued work force…

2 Paraphrase these sentences 1–3.

1 The volcanic eruption devastated the surrounding countryside, killing many people.

2 Share prices rose in the first quarter, leading analysts to predict even more growth later in the year.

3 The film's director told the press that this would be his final film.

Get writing

Sometimes we need to summarize a sequence of events, rather than another piece of writing. For example, if we need to report a crime to the police, or if we want to describe something we learnt to someone who wasn't there. These summaries should contain enough detail for the reader to understand exactly what happened.

1 Your colleague Jane has had an accident at work. You need to summarize the sequence of events for an accident report. Use the notes below to write your summary. Write in complete sentences and use the past tense.

Jane arrives 7.45am (early). Cleaner still washing floor in hall. Jane stops to talk to Bill (night security guard) at reception. She asks abt. his holiday. Checks watch -> realizes nearly 8am, gathers briefcase + papers, runs to lift. J slips on floor, falls awkwardly onto her side -> drops her stuff. Sec. guard + cleaner come over to help - J holding her left shoulder/unable to move arm. As sec. guard finishing at 8am, he drives J to hospital for immediate check. J only has bruise on upper arm - no broken bones.

USEFUL TIPS

Here are some steps to follow before you begin writing your summary.

1 Skim-read your source text. How many paragraphs are there? Does each paragraph contain a main idea? What is it? Take notes on the structure of the article – these notes are called an outline.

2 Read the source text again carefully. Underline any new words and look these up in a dictionary. Re-read until everything makes sense. Decide which details you need to include in your summary; it should not include every fact or idea in the source text – only the main ones are necessary.

3 Check your notes. Do you have enough information to write your summary? Do you know roughly how long your summary will be and how many paragraphs it will have? Do you have an idea for a thesis statement and a list of main points? If not, go back and read the source text once again.

Once you are ready to being writing your summary, there are some more steps to follow:

4 Start with your thesis statement. Make sure that it sums up the main idea or ideas in the source text.

5 Using the structure from your notes, begin writing the rest of the summary. If it is only one or two paragraphs long, the main ideas can each be summed up in a sentence or two. If it is a longer summary, one short paragraph for each main idea is good.

6 Finally, check that your sentences are sufficiently different from those in the source text. If they aren't, paraphrase more!

2 **Find a text of more than 200 words and write a summary of it.**
- Take notes on the main point or points of the article.
- Write a thesis statement and begin your summary with it.
- Divide your summary into paragraphs if you need to, but keep it short.
- Remember to paraphrase the article – don't copy any of the sentences you read.

There is an example text and a model answer in the Answer key.

12 WRITING AN ARTICLE OR ESSAY

It is likely that, at some point, you will have to write an extended text in a magazine or newspaper style, or you may have to write an essay as part of your studies. Whether writing an essay or article for a course tutor, for your workplace newsletter or for a personal blog, it is important to plan what your article or essay will cover before you start writing, and to structure your writing into paragraphs. This will help organize your thoughts and will help make your writing clear, interesting and memorable.

Understanding

Read the article below. How is it structured? How does this help you to read it?

How to lower your grocery bills

The best thing to do if you want to save money on your grocery bills is to think ahead. That way, you can plan your meals for the week and list all the ingredients you will need to make them. This prevents expensive, last-minute trips to the supermarket for one dinner ingredient. You are far more likely to buy unnecessary items when you are in a rush.

Many consumers make savings by shopping online. Despite the fact that there is usually a delivery charge for online grocery deliveries, many people find online shopping saves both time and money. Impulse buys are easier to resist and bargains are often easier to spot. In addition, simply because consumers can see their bill adding up as they shop, they are far more likely to stick to the budget they intended.

Many consumers are finding that rising fuel costs are adding to their shopping bills, because they are driving miles away to shop at a 'cheaper' supermarket. Another option is to consider shopping locally.

It is worthwhile checking the prices in your high street and calculating how much you could save by walking home with your shopping! Moreover, you will be supporting your own community too.

None of these tactics will work, however, unless you actually monitor your total household spending. To tightly control your spending, consider moving to online banking, where you can check your bank accounts daily, move money, and avoid costly bank charges as well.

Discourse markers

One important way to structure an essay or article is to use discourse markers – words or phrases that link ideas within a text.

Discourse markers can be grouped according to their function. Some connect similar ideas within a text:

*Shopping online can save you money. **Furthermore**, it can save you time.*

*Recycling means that less waste goes to landfill sites. **Moreover**, it benefits the economy.*

***In addition** to the ideas already mentioned, you can also…*

Other discourse markers can be used to show two contrasting points:

The rise in house prices has made it difficult for young people to afford a home.
***On the other hand**, it has made some homeowners very wealthy.*

***Although** the latest generation of smartphones have excellent cameras, their battery life is poor.*

***In spite of** the mud and rain, festival-goers had an excellent time.*

***Despite** the environmental impact of driving, many people continue to buy new cars.*

*I enjoyed the band's new single. **However**, it wasn't as good as their previous one.*

Language focus

1 **Look through the article again. Underline the discourse markers.**

2 **Complete sentences 1–4 using discourse markers:**

1 .... it means taking time to plan ahead, working out your shopping in advance can save you money.

2 .... the delivery charges, many people choose to shop online.

3 You should monitor your total budget to save money. ...., you should consider using online banking.

4 Supermarkets on the edge of town are often cheaper. ...., it costs money to travel there and back.

Topic sentences

A good way to help your readers understand your article or essay is to use topic sentences in each paragraph. A topic sentence generally appears near the beginning of each paragraph and sums up what that paragraph is about. It helps the reader to predict what is coming, and to relate that to what they have already read. This is particularly helpful as readers often skim read through long texts to get the basic idea.

Looking more closely

Read through the article once more. Underline the topic sentence in each paragraph.

Example

Paragraph 1: <u>The best thing to do if you want to save money on your grocery bills is to think ahead</u>.

Writing clearly

Write a topic sentence for each paragraph of the following article:

Article title: Why we should eat fruit and vegetables at every meal

Paragraph 1: Introduction.

Paragraph 2: Some issues with eating fruit and vegetables at every meal.

Paragraph 3: The good things about eating fruit and vegetables at every meal.

Paragraph 4: Conclusion.

Writing appropriately

1 **Take another look at the article on page 48. Why is it divided into four paragraphs?**

Paragraphs

Why should we use paragraphs? Paragraphs are important because they break a long text into manageable sections. Try reading a long passage of text without paragraphs and you will soon lose your place and get frustrated. Paragraphs, like sentences, give us natural breaks in which to process the information we have read.

How do we know when to start a new paragraph? This is a difficult skill to master at first. Some texts use many short paragraphs, others use fewer and longer paragraphs. A general rule is that we should start a new paragraph when the subject of the text changes, or when we are introducing a new idea.

Each paragraph should contain a topic sentence, followed by a number of supporting sentences that develop the main idea in a topic sentence.

2 **Read the following sentences, which make up two paragraphs. Decide where one paragraph ends and the other starts. Identify the topic sentences and supporting sentences.**

The number of printed newspapers sold in the UK has fallen dramatically in recent years. This has mainly been due to the popularity of online news sources, which are generally free to access. In addition, many people now get their news from social media sources such as Twitter. In spite of the shift to online news, many people continue to purchase printed newspapers and magazines. Some have even increased their circulation, perhaps because of the perception that online news sources are unreliable.

3 **Think about the following article titles. How would you structure them into paragraphs?**

  1 Scientists predict time travel will be possible for humans

  2 New smartphones are not as great as everyone thinks

USEFUL TIPS

- One way to ensure that you write a good essay or article is to make a careful plan before you start. Without a plan it is easy to get lost, repeat ideas, write too much or too little.
- Start your plan by thinking about your audience. Who will read it? What will they be interested in? How much time will they have to read it? A tutor reading an essay or article for a course will have very different expectations from a colleague reading a blog article of yours, for example.
- Are you presenting facts, an argument, or something else? Generally, all articles and essays benefit from having a clear introduction and conclusion. However, an essay that contains an argument needs to clearly separate the points for and against the argument. An article that presents facts needs to be structured logically. Is there a timeline you could follow, or can the facts be separated into different groups?
- Pay attention to the language you choose. Try to avoid using complex vocabulary or technical jargon unless you are certain your readers will understand it. Avoid using informal language or slang in essays and more formal articles.

Get writing

Your boss has asked you to write an article on 'What you should consider before moving abroad'.

- First, plan your article. You are writing for an English speaking audience, aged from 16–60. The article should be around 300 words long. It should include an introduction and conclusion with several paragraphs in between.
- Now ask yourself 'What would I consider if I was thinking of moving abroad?' Take some notes on the most obvious questions you would want answers to. These will help you with your research. They could also form the paragraph structure for your article.
- Next, carry out your research in order to write supporting sentences for each paragraph in your article. You can type the questions you identified straight into a search engine. Try to look through a number of sources of information and to double-check any facts. Avoid cutting and pasting text straight from the Internet. Instead, type up notes in your own words.
- Finally, proofread your article and make any necessary changes.

13 WRITING FORMAL NOTES AND NOTICES

There may be occasions when you become part of a formal group or committee. Perhaps you may become a volunteer warden in a student residence, or take part in a community group that looks after a neighbourhood. When you take up positions of responsibility like these, you might be asked to write notes (or minutes) at meetings, or write notices or newsletters about your group's activities.

Understanding

Read the public notice below. What is the purpose of the notice?

> ### Notice to Residents
>
> Warning! There have been some thefts from houses in this area in the past month. Residents are reminded of some simple precautions to prevent crime:
> - Lock all doors and windows, even if you going out for only a short while.
> - If you are going away on holiday, ask a neighbour to keep an eye on your house while you are away.
> - Keep all valuable items away from windows where they can be easily seen.
> - If you see anyone acting strangely, do not hesitate to contact the police.
>
> Your neighbourhood welfare committee was established in 2010 to help ensure a safe and happy neighbourhood for everyone who lives here. We meet monthly in the Community Centre and all residents are invited to attend. If you have any questions, please contact us.
>
> Tel: Nissa Laarsen 01271 447 889
> Email: communitygroup@barnstaplewest.org.uk
> Meeting minutes can be downloaded from
> www.barnstaplewest-communitygroup.co.uk.

Looking more closely

Take another look at the notice. What can you say about (1) the author, (2) the structure and (3) where you might see a notice like this?

The passive

The passive voice is a grammatical structure which we sometimes use in formal writing, especially when we want to focus our readers' attention on the action of a sentence and not on the person or people carrying out the action.

*All thefts **will be reported** to the police.*

In this sentence, the actors (people who steal) are not mentioned. Instead, the action of the sentence (reporting their crimes to the police) is the focus of the sentence. To form a passive sentence we use: a form of the verb 'to be' + past participle. If we need to include the actor(s) in a passive sentence, we can do so using 'by'.

The local neighbourhood welfare committee prepared this notice.

⇒ *This notice **was prepared by** the local neighbourhood welfare committee.*

Language focus

1. **Read the notice again and underline sentences that are written in the passive.**

2. **Change the active sentences 1–3 into the passive:**

   1 Thieves have broken into some houses in the neighbourhood.

   2 Marcia White wrote this notice.

   3 The Council have placed extra rubbish bins around the park.

USEFUL TIPS

- It is common to use 'we', 'our' and 'us' when writing a notice for a group (rather than using 'I', 'my' and 'me'. This tells the reader that the group is made up of a number of members and gives the notice more authority.
- Avoid using slang, abbreviations or colloquial language; it gives readers the impression that the notice isn't serious.
- That said, public notices need to be clear and easy to understand. Some of your readers may not speak fluent English, or may be quite young, so keep language simple.
- People don't usually have time to read long notices, so include only the most important information.
- Try to print your notices in as large a font as possible, to attract attention and to help readers who have poor eyesight. Make your heading really stand out so people can read it from a distance.

Writing appropriately

Minutes are a formal record of what was discussed and decided at a meeting.

Read the minutes printed below. Label the sections a-e in the order they appear:

a   .... The items on the meeting agenda followed by discussion points.

b   .... Anything that wasn't listed on the original agenda.

c   .... The list of people who attended the meeting.

d   .... The title, purpose and date of the meeting.

e   .... Name(s) of people who couldn't attend the meeting.

Richmond Hall Student Residences Committee Meeting: 26 October 2012

Reason for meeting: Richmond Hall End of Term Christmas Ball
Committee members attending: Michael Norman, Bianca Ortega,
Sean McCarthy, Jo Averbach Apologies: Renee Girard.

1. First Agenda Item: Date for the Christmas Ball

Discussion points:
- Marc and Jo were worried about noise levels during the
  Christmas ball for those students who have rooms are above
  the dining room, where the dinner and dancing will be held.
- Bianca stated that all lectures are scheduled to end on Tuesday
  20 December, so very few students would have essay deadlines
  to meet over the weekend of 17 and 18 December.

Decision: It was decided that Friday 16 December would be the most
appropriate date for the ball.

2. Second Agenda Item: Catering for the Christmas Ball

Discussion points:
- It had become clear to the Committee that students were
  prepared to pay more for their Ball ticket if this meant that
  they could have outside catering.
- Three different catering companies were asked to provide
  quotes. Top Table Catering provided both the cheapest quote
  and most attractive menu.

Decision: Top Table's 'Four course gala menu' was selected as the most
appropriate for the event.

3. Any other business: Next meeting 9 November 2012

- Suggested agenda items: 1. Final choice of band 2. Ticket Price
  3. Publicity
- Any other agenda items are welcomed: please give them to
  Michael before 7/11/2012.

USEFUL TIPS

There is not a set way of structuring minutes, although they usually have the following elements in common:

- Minutes generally follow the meeting agenda (a list of the things to be discussed at the meeting, which is sent to each group member in advance) in the same order as they are listed on the agenda.
- The person writing the minutes needs to summarize the important discussion points, noting down suggestions and who agrees and who disagrees with them. If any decision is taken or if someone is given a task to perform, this should be recorded carefully.
- The final agenda item is usually to make a plan for the next meeting, or to create an agenda for the next meeting. If a date or tasks for the next meeting are set, these need to be recorded.
- Sometimes there is a general agenda item called 'Any other business' (AOB), in which group members can raise any questions not listed on the agenda.

Get writing

1. The wheelie (rubbish) bins in your neighbourhood are being vandalized. Write a public notice to invite local residents to a meeting. Summarize the problem, give details of when and where to meet, and include contact details.

2. Try to remember a meeting you have attended recently. Take some minutes from memory. Alternatively, look for a meeting that will take place in your neighbourhood soon, and practise taking minutes while you are listening. Another alternative is to have a discussion with friends or family about a task you need to complete. Take some minutes to record who was there and what was said.

- Note the date and purpose of the meeting.
- Remember to list the people present at the discussion and anyone missing.
- List the points discussed in order. Note down any differences of opinion.
- List any decisions made or tasks and who has agreed to do them.
- If you wrote the minutes by hand, type them up and send them to the group (if appropriate).

14 A LETTER OR EMAIL OF COMPLAINT

Sometimes, when we have experienced poor service or bought something that doesn't work, talking about the problem to the person or company responsible isn't enough. In many cases, companies will take a written complaint much more seriously than a verbal one, and writing a good letter of complaint may help you to resolve the issue

Understanding

Read the email below. Decide if the statements 1–4 are true or false:

	True	False
1 The tone of the letter is polite, but not friendly or light-hearted	—	—
2 It is factual and very formal and clearly expresses disappointment.	—	—
3 The first paragraph summarizes the complaint in detail.	—	—
4 The letter contains praise of the restaurant.	—	—

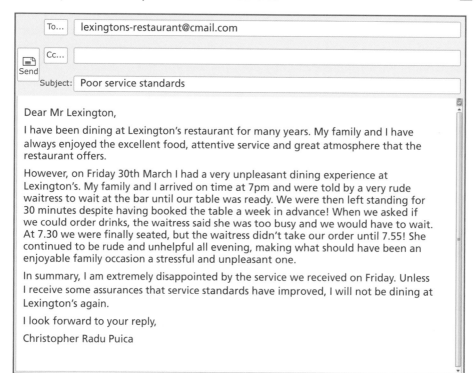

To... lexingtons-restaurant@cmail.com

Cc...

Send

Subject: Poor service standards

Dear Mr Lexington,

I have been dining at Lexington's restaurant for many years. My family and I have always enjoyed the excellent food, attentive service and great atmosphere that the restaurant offers.

However, on Friday 30th March I had a very unpleasant dining experience at Lexington's. My family and I arrived on time at 7pm and were told by a very rude waitress to wait at the bar until our table was ready. We were then left standing for 30 minutes despite having booked the table a week in advance! When we asked if we could order drinks, the waitress said she was too busy and we would have to wait. At 7.30 we were finally seated, but the waitress didn't take our order until 7.55! She continued to be rude and unhelpful all evening, making what should have been an enjoyable family occasion a stressful and unpleasant one.

In summary, I am extremely disappointed by the service we received on Friday. Unless I receive some assurances that service standards have improved, I will not be dining at Lexington's again.

I look forward to your reply,

Christopher Radu Puica

Expressing opinions

In a letter of complaint, it is perfectly acceptable to describe how the poor service or product made you feel. Doing so shows the reader how important the subject is to you and helps them understand why you are complaining. Saying how you felt is not the same as being rude. Compare the following sentences to see the difference:

1 *Your restaurant is terrible! The staff are mean and the food is disgusting!* (This sentence is rude and sounds exaggerated.)

2 *I was very disappointed by the meal I had at your restaurant last Tuesday. Two of the waiting staff were rude and one of our meals was cold and tasteless.* (This sentence focuses on the writer's experience, not on attacking the reader. It refers to specific problems, rather than making general statements which are hard to prove.)

Here are some useful phrases for expressing opinions when complaining:

Phrases to show that you are normally used to better service:

Until recently, I have enjoyed ...

... has always been excellent. Recently however, ...

I was surprised to experience ...

Phrases to express disappointment:

I was (extremely) disappointed to ...

I am (very) disappointed in ...

I expect a much higher standard of service from ...

Phrases to ask for a resolution to a problem:

Unless (X happens), I (will/won't do X ...)
Because of X, I expect you to ...
Due to X, I ask/request that you ...

Writing appropriately

1 **Read the email again. Underline the words and phrases that express opinions.**

2 **Match the sentence halves 1–6 and a–f.**

1 I was very disappointed by
2 I expect a much higher standard of service
3 Until recently I have been
4 Unless I receive an apology
5 Because your food was off
6 Due to the fault with my TV,

a a big fan of your service.
b I won't be returning to your store.
c the service I received at your café.
d I experienced food poisoning.
e from your shop.
f I ask that you replace it quickly.

3 **Write some sentences to express your opinion in the following situations 1–3:**

1 Your telephone banking service, which is normally good, is now causing you problems.

2 You bought a very expensive bicycle, only to find that parts of it are badly damaged.

3 You were insulted by an assistant in a clothes shop and you want an apology.

Language focus

1. **Read the email on page 56 once more. How does the writer communicate what the waitress said to him and his family? Underline the sentences.**

Reported speech

When we want to tell someone what someone else said to us but we can't remember the exact words, we can use reported speech. Reported speech is useful when complaining, because complaints often involve things that were said or promised to us verbally. For example:

> *I was told by your manager that I could have a refund.*
>
> *Your shop assistant said that I couldn't return the dress.*
>
> *The person I spoke to promised they would sort this out.*

When we write reported speech (also called indirect speech) there are a few things to remember:

- We don't need to use quotation marks.
- We do need to use a reporting verb, such as 'said', 'told' or 'promised'.
- When reporting something that was said to us in the past, we need to change the verbs to the past tense (for example, *'You'll have to wait.'* becomes: *He told me I would have to wait.*).
- Pronouns need to change too (for example, *'You can't have a refund.'* becomes: *She said I couldn't have a refund.*).

2. **Turn these examples of direct speech 1–4 into reported speech:**

1. Man: 'There's nothing wrong with your washing machine.'
2. Woman: 'I can't help you with your problem.'
3. Man: 'I'm too busy to serve you. You'll have to wait.'
4. Woman: 'I promise I'll get someone to call you back soon.'

Get writing

1. **Make these rude sentences 1–3 polite and more informative. Add details if necessary.**

Example   *Your restaurant is terrible!*
> ⇒ *I am very disappointed with the service I received at your restaurant on Friday 4th March.*

1. Your customer service representatives are all liars!
2. The sandwich I ate made me so ill I thought I was going to die! Your restaurant is dirty and dangerous!
3. I can't believe how long it is taking you to refund the money you owe me. If you don't sort this out by tomorrow, I will take legal action!

2 Write a letter of complaint (not an email) about a banking or financial services problem:

- Include your address, the date and the address of the company you are writing to. Remember that your address should go on the top right of the letter page. The date should appear under your address. The company address should appear under the date, but on the left side of the letter page.
- Use 'Dear sir/madam' if you don't know the name of the person you are writing to.
- Add a subject line that refers to the account or other details which identify you as a customer. For example, a bank account number followed by a short sentence about the problem. This allows the reader to quickly identify the problem, and to look up your details in their system.
- Describe the problem in detail. If you have already phoned or written about the problem, explain when and what was said.
- Be polite, but explain how the problem has made you feel.
- Say how you want the problem to be resolved.
- Finish with 'yours faithfully' and your full name.

USEFUL TIPS

- A common mistake when complaining is to get overly emotional or to exaggerate what happened. If you do this, your reader may not take your letter very seriously. Of course a restaurant is not terrible just because you had one bad meal there, even if it may feel that way.
- Be truthful. If only one waiter was rude, don't write 'your staff are rude'.
- If you are normally used to better service or products from a company, say so. It tells the reader that you are a valuable customer and that you care about their company.
- When you are writing a letter of complaint, it is particularly important to ensure that you thoroughly check your letter for errors. A letter that is free of mistakes will have much more impact than one which is carelessly written. For tips on proofreading, see p97.

  If you need to write more than one letter, always refer to any previous letters you have written, including the date you sent them and whether or not you received a response.
- It is very helpful to keep copies of any complaint letters that you write. In this way, you can check your records if the issue remains unresolved for a long time. If the company offers you a solution, you can also check back to ensure that all your concerns have been addressed, the company should mention each point that you made in your original complaint letter, offering an answer to each.
- Keep copies of the complaint letters that got the result you wanted, this will help you write any new letters you need to write in future!

15 APPLYING FOR A JOB: YOUR CV

BEFORE YOU START

Most employers want to see your CV (= curriculum vitae, known as a *résumé* in American English). Your CV is a summary of your education, skills and work experience, plus your contact details. It may open with a personal statement. Your CV should give employers the information they need to decide if you are right for a job.

Writing clearly

1 **Read Agata's CV opposite. Complete it with the headings that are listed in the box below, paying attention to the order in which they appear on Agata's CV.**

> Education/Qualifications   Work Experience   Skills   Personal statement   Referees

2 **In her CV, Agata uses different adjectives to describe her personal qualities and skills. Find and circle the adjectives.**

Example: I am an(experienced)waitress.

Choosing adjectives for your CV

- Adjectives such as *skilled*, *professional* and *hardworking* tell an employer about your personal qualities. They describe what kind of person you *are*, rather than what you can *do*.
- It's important to choose adjectives that describe you accurately. If you say you are reliable, make sure you can give examples to prove it.
- Try to use a variety of adjectives in your CV. Simply repeating that you are a 'good' communicator and 'good at' customer service doesn't tell an employer very much.

Writing a personal statement for your CV

A personal statement is a paragraph that summarizes your skills and personal qualities. Not all CVs include them, but they can be a useful way to catch an employer's attention. They also add a personal touch to a document that can otherwise seem like a rather dull list.

A personal statement should be short (less than 100 words). It should be written in complete sentences, not bullet points or a list. You should use adjectives that describe the personal qualities that make you suitable for the job you are applying for.

Agata Nowak

Flat 2a, 12 Middlemarch Road,
London SW17 4ES
0776588347
agy.nowak@dmail.com

1 ....

Currently studying English in London, I am looking for part-time work in a challenging customer service role. An experienced waitress and shop assistant, I am versatile, reliable and polite. I enjoy busy and demanding jobs and look forward to learning more new skills.

2 ....

2011 Certificate of English (Upper Intermediate)
Princes College, Fulham

2007–2010 Maturity Certificate,
Wroclaw Technical College

3 ....

2009–2010 Counter Assistant,
Mode Fashions, Wroclaw
I kept this popular shop tidy, attractive and well stocked at all times, served customers and worked on the till.

2007–2009 Waitress,
Condor Café, Wroclaw
I served customers, cleaned tables and also helped in the kitchen of this busy restaurant.

4 ....

- Confident English speaker (Upper Intermediate level).
- Fluent in Polish and German. An able communicator and enthusiastic team member.
- Excellent customer service skills.
- Competent in all Microsoft Office® software.
- Attained Level 2 Award in Food Hygiene & Safety for Catering (2011).

5 ....

Mrs Katherine Chapman,
Senior Teacher of English,
Princes College, Fulham
k.chapman@princesfulham.co.uk
0208 443 6767

Mr Aleksandr Zawadzki,
Manager, Mode Fashions,
Wroclaw
a.zawadzki@mode.pl
+48 67 665 5892

Looking more closely

Read each example of a personal quality 1–5, then write another sentence to show what it means.

1 I am very reliable. *I always come to work on time.*

2 I am an experienced office worker. ....

3 I am hardworking. ....

4 I am professional. ....

5 I am skilled with computers. ....

Language note

When we write about work experience, we use the simple present tense or present continuous to talk about the job we are doing now. To save space, we write short sentences and sometimes miss out the subject of the sentence (I) and start with the verb.

Examples   *(I) provide support to a team of nurses.*
Providing support to a team of nurses.

When we talk about jobs we did in the past, we use the simple past tense.

Examples   *(I) served customers; (I) worked on the till; (I) cleaned tables.*

Language focus

1 **Complete the descriptions 2–10 with verbs from the box. Change each verb to the simple past tense.**

1 ..*Helped*.. school children with their reading.

2 .... questions from museum visitors.

3 .... reports and .... filing in the office.

4 .... a tractor and helped to feed farm animals.

5 .... customers in the restaurant.

6 .... sandwiches and desserts in the kitchen.

7 .... boxes and crates in the delivery department.

8 .... letters and parcels to local residents.

9 .... French and Italian to adults at evening classes.

10 .... documents from Hungarian to Spanish.

drive	
	help
do	
	serve
answer	
	write
translate	
	deliver
teach	
	prepare
pack	

2 **Write a sentence describing the main responsibilities of each job 2–5 below. Use the present continuous tense.**

1   Language teacher

Teaching classes and helping students with their language skills.
....

2   Waiter/Waitress

....

3   Book shop assistant

....

4   Cleaner

....

5   Restaurant manager

....

Get writing

1 **Write your personal statement.**

2 **Now write the rest of your CV. Before you start, review all the advice in this unit, and look at Agata's CV again.**

USEFUL TIPS

- Be concise. Try to keep your CV short. However, if you are applying for a graduate job that requires a lot of experience, a longer CV may be acceptable.
- If you aren't sure what to include, ask. Read the job advertisement carefully. If that doesn't help, call the company and ask what they need to know. Big companies will have an HR (= human resources) department who can advise you.
- Use a spellcheck and re-read your CV several times before you send it. Employers often receive lots of CVs, so even a small mistake can count against you!
  If you don't have much work experience, consider including an 'Achievements' section, to show employers some of the important things you have done, for example:

Achievements

- Won national synchronized swimming contest three years in a row.
- Was promoted twice in my first year at High Street Bank.
- Completed the London Marathon, raising £3,000 for charity.

16 APPLYING FOR A JOB: YOUR COVERING LETTER

When you apply for a job you will normally send a covering letter with your CV. This is true whether you apply by post or by email. Your covering letter helps you to 'advertise' yourself and adds a personal touch to your application. A good covering letter will emphasize your most relevant skills in a way that your CV can't, and can persuade an employer that you are the right person for the job.

Understanding

1. **Read the covering letter for a bar job that is shown opposite.**
   - What's in the subject line?
   - What is the function of the first line of the covering letter?
   - What does the first full paragraph then tell you about Madeleine?
   - What does Madeleine explain in her second paragraph?
   - How does Madeleine complete her covering letter?

2. **Read Madeleine's covering letter again. Answer questions 1–4:**
   1. How did Madeleine hear about the job?
   2. What relevant experience does she mention?
   3. What might make Madeleine's letter stand out?
   4. Why does she think she is suitable for this role?

Writing appropriately

Which of the following would you include in a covering letter?
- Details of your school exam grades.
- A summary of your work experience.
- Your address.
- Your age.
- Why you want to leave your current job.
- Your present salary.

To...	dragonflies@cmail.com
Cc...	

Send

Subject: Full-time Bar Manager, Dragonflies Bar-Restaurant: Madeleine Michel

Dear Mr Gregory,

I am applying for the post of Full-time Bar Manager, as advertised in *The List* on Friday 1 March.

I am an experienced and versatile bar person, having worked in the industry for the past five years in a number of increasingly responsible roles. I am currently Assistant Bar Manager at the bar-restaurant Olive, where I not only helped hire, train and manage a team of enthusiastic young bar people, but created a popular cocktails list to complement our food menu. As a direct result, Olive recently won an award for its cocktail innovation. I have really enjoyed working in such a demanding and rewarding role; nevertheless I feel that I am more than ready to meet the challenge of running a city-centre bar single-handed.

Because of my experience and drive, and since I have worked in a wide range of bar-restaurants, I believe that I have what it takes to successfully manage Dragonflies Bar-Restaurant and develop it into an even more profitable business. I would welcome the opportunity to prove my knowledge and ability in such an exciting new environment. Therefore, I would be very grateful if you would consider my application. My CV is attached, in pdf format as requested.

I very much look forward to hearing from you,

Madeleine Michel

USEFUL TIPS

- A good covering letter will give a summary of your most relevant experience and achievements, without repeating all the detail of your CV. Remember that this is a letter, not an essay.
- Your covering letter must show how you are different from other applicants, and it must show why you want this particular job (and not just any job). Before you write your covering letter, do some research on the company you are applying to. Use your research to explain why you want to work there.
- It is usually a good idea to briefly mention why you are applying for a new job, but be careful. If you hate your present job, that is not a good thing to put in a covering letter. Employers want to know that you really want to work for them, not that you are trying to get away from somewhere else!

Language focus

1 **Read the covering letter on page 65 again. Identify the words and phrases that connect one idea to another.**

In a covering letter, we can use connecting words to show how our experience and skills relate to the job description.

Example   *Because of my experience with ... I feel I'd make an excellent ...*

Other connecting words and phrases should how our actions caused a successful result, making us a more appealing applicant:

Example   *I revised our workflow processes, and as a result, productivity improved.*

2 **Complete the sentences 1–5 with suitable connecting words from the box. More than one answer may be correct.**

1 .... of my revisions to the menu, more customers came to the café.

2 .... did profitability improve, but my team were happier too.

3 .... that I have worked in the industry for over 5 years, I believe I have the necessary experience for this role.

4 I am applying to your company .... I believe in your values and admire your history.

5 I hired and trained two new staff. ...., efficiency was increased by 50%.

consequently
because
due to the fact
serve
as a result
not only

Some common mistakes with covering letters

- Writing too much information: recruiters are often too busy to read long covering letters.
- Getting the name of the company, the manager or the job wrong: this is usually an excuse for employers to dismiss your application completely! Check and double-check.
- Spelling and grammatical errors: with spell-checking software, there is no excuse for this.
- Not saying why you want to work for that company: your covering letter needs to be targeted, not general.
- Cutting and pasting text from another application: this tells employers you are careless and not very interested in them.
- Not following the instructions in the advertisement: some companies ask applicants for a hand-written covering letter. If you write your letter by hand, make sure that it is very clear and easy to read. If the employer does not specify a hand-written letter, you may type it, but choose your font carefully (usually a fairly traditional style) and lay your letter out clearly.

Language note

Taking the initiative in applying for a job can be hard. It is difficult to know what to write to someone you have never met, about a job you may know very little about. Here are some helpful phrases for sounding confident in your covering letter.

To start:

> *I am applying for the position of ..., which I saw advertised ... on ...*

> *write in response to your job advertisement, as seen on ...*

To show how you meet the job requirements:

> *I have 3 years' experience as leader of a productive and successful call centre team.*

> *I'm a capable, professional waitress, with wide-ranging experience of the catering industry including: ...*

> *In my time at Company X, I increased profitability/reduced waiting times/ helped my company win an award ...*

To say why you want a new job:

> *After three years in my present job, I feel it is time to take on a new challenge.*

> *Having finished my degree I am seeking a role that utilizes all of my skills.*

To close:

> *I would welcome the opportunity to discuss my suitability for this role in person.*

> *I attach my CV in support of my application.*

> *I look forward to hearing from you.*

Get writing

Look for a job advertisement online or in a local paper. Find one that matches your skills and experience. Write a covering letter.

- Make it clear which job you are applying for.
- Check you have the contact details and job title correct.
- Summarize the relevant experience from your CV, but don't repeat all the detail.
- Say why you are applying for this job.
- Include some information that makes you stand out from other applicants.

17 TRAVEL BLOGGING

Have you ever travelled somewhere amazing? How did you share stories of your trip with friends? Travel blogs are usually written by people who are going on long and interesting journeys; or by people who have moved to a new and interesting country. A travel blog serves many purposes: it gives you a written record of your travels; it allows family and friends to follow your progress; and it opens the world of travel to a wider audience – you never know who might be reading!

Understanding

Read the two blog entries below. What is the blog about? Where does the writer go?

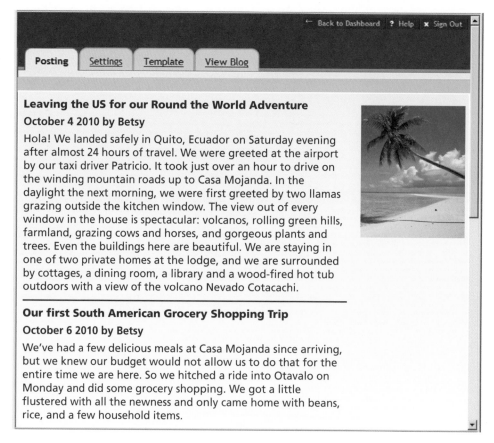

← Back to Dashboard   ? Help   ✕ Sign Out

| Posting | Settings | Template | View Blog |

Leaving the US for our Round the World Adventure

October 4 2010 by Betsy

Hola! We landed safely in Quito, Ecuador on Saturday evening after almost 24 hours of travel. We were greeted at the airport by our taxi driver Patricio. It took just over an hour to drive on the winding mountain roads up to Casa Mojanda. In the daylight the next morning, we were first greeted by two llamas grazing outside the kitchen window. The view out of every window in the house is spectacular: volcanos, rolling green hills, farmland, grazing cows and horses, and gorgeous plants and trees. Even the buildings here are beautiful. We are staying in one of two private homes at the lodge, and we are surrounded by cottages, a dining room, a library and a wood-fired hot tub outdoors with a view of the volcano Nevado Cotacachi.

Our first South American Grocery Shopping Trip

October 6 2010 by Betsy

We've had a few delicious meals at Casa Mojanda since arriving, but we knew our budget would not allow us to do that for the entire time we are here. So we hitched a ride into Otavalo on Monday and did some grocery shopping. We got a little flustered with all the newness and only came home with beans, rice, and a few household items.

Language note

A person who writes a blog is called a 'blogger'.

Writing a blog is called 'blogging'.

'Blog' is both a noun and a verb:

> *Betsy writes a travel blog.*

> *Betsy blogs about her travels.*

Writing appropriately

1 **Read the blog again. What words and phrases does Betsy use to describe the places she visits?**

Describing places

The best travel blogs are full of rich descriptions that make it easy for you to imagine the places the writer is visiting. One of the best ways to make your writing more descriptive is to use adjectives. Compare these two sentences:

> *We drove up the hill to Casa Mojanda.*

> *We drove up the steep and winding hills to beautiful Casa Mojanda.*

Another technique is to describe what you can see around you (or what you can remember seeing if you aren't there any more).

> *In the daylight the next morning, we were first greeted by two llamas grazing outside the kitchen window.*

Using metaphors is another good way to 'paint a picture' in your reader's mind.

> *The crafts market was an explosion of colour.*

A metaphor is when you use one thing (like an explosion) to represent an idea or image (for example that the market was extremely colourful, as though there had been an explosion in a paint factory!)

2 **Think about the last journey you made. Follow these instructions:**

a Write a basic sentence about it. (Example: *I took the bus home to Vauxhall.*)

b Add some adjectives to make the sentence descriptive. (Example: *I took the creaky old bus home to sleepy Vauxhall.*)

c Say what you could see on your journey. (Example: *From the bus I saw people trudging home, hiding under their umbrellas.*)

d Now add a metaphor. (Example: *The sky was a frown of grey clouds.*)

3 Read the blog post below. How does the author indicate that something particularly special has happened?

Home   About   Gallery

Blog post

Recent posts

Seeing the Amazon for the first time

October 2 2012 by Wanderguy

Back at the airport today, this time for our flight to Iquitos. There were perhaps only a hundred seats on the plane, mostly taken up by Peruvian families. The flight was spectacular. I've travelled to many beautiful places before, and enjoyed a few stunning flights too, but nothing had prepared me for my first sight of the Amazon. The golden, sand-coloured river snakes through its rainforest home in an amazing contrast of colour. I've never seen anything like it and I will remember it forever.

Blog roll

Language focus

1 Contrast these two sentences from the blog post. What tense are they in? Why?

The flight was spectacular.

I've never seen anything like It ...

Past simple or present perfect?

We use the past simple to talk about completed actions in the past.

We were met at the airport by our bad-tempered taxi driver.

We use the present perfect tense to talk about our experiences – though they include events that happened in the past, our experiences allow us to observe things that are still relevant now. In this way, the present perfect describes a situation that began in the past and is still happening or still true today.

I've been to some crazy cities before, but Lima must surely be the craziest!

2 **Answer the questions 1–3 in the present perfect:**

1 What's the most amazing thing you've ever seen?

2 What's the most memorable journey you've ever taken?

3 What's the craziest place you've ever visited?

Get writing

Think of an interesting journey you have made and write a couple of blog posts about it.

Before you write, jot down the ideas for the following questions:

- What will interest your reader?
- What is different from home?
- What are the people like?
- What is the lifestyle like?
- What does it look, smell and sound like?

USEFUL TIPS

- How is a travel blog different from other blogs?
  The content should be focused on the travel, journey or culture in the place being visited. This can include all kinds of stories. A blog about your trip to the bank at home would be boring, but a blog about your trip to the bank in an unfamiliar culture could be very interesting.

- How often should you blog?
  Blog too often and your audience will lose interest and start skipping your posts. Blog too infrequently and readers will lose interest and drift away. Choose a frequency you feel comfortable with and try to stick with it. For example, a quick post with a photo every couple of days, or a longer post once a week are both manageable.

- How do you stay motivated?
  Blogging shouldn't be a chore. At first it can be exciting to see your stories online, but after a few weeks you may run out of ideas and feel less enthusiastic. The trick is to keep going. If you think of a good idea for a blog, note it down and write up your ideas as soon as you can. Write to entertain yourself, not just your readers.

18 TWEETING

BEFORE YOU START

Do you follow anyone on Twitter? Do you Tweet or not? Perhaps you use Twitter as a way of catching up with current affairs, or to read about your favourite celebrities. However you use it, Twitter is becoming an important presence in English Language. Practically everybody who is 'somebody' writes there, using a very specific style of writing known as 'Tweeting'. Understanding how Tweeting works and writing your own Tweets can be great fun. Moreover, reading and writing Tweets will give you a great insight into contemporary, informal English.

Understanding

Read the tweets below. What is their purpose?

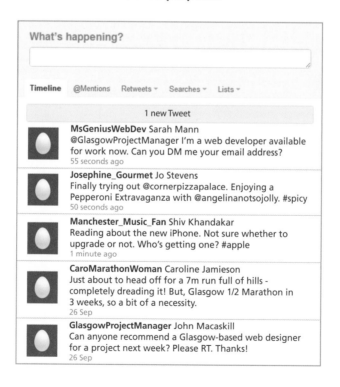

Writing appropriately

If you are new to Twitter, there is some important terminology to learn before you start:

- A 'Tweet' is a message that you write and share on Twitter. It must be no longer than 140 characters.
- To 'Tweet' is to publish a message on Twitter.
- A person who tweets is called a 'Tweeter' or a 'Twitterer'.
- On Twitter you can choose to 'follow' people: friends, celebrities, journalists, brands, even strangers. When you follow someone you become their 'follower'. If they follow you back then they become your follower too.

To get something from Twitter you need to do two things: one is to follow people who interest you, the other is to Tweet. Unlike in real life, on Twitter it is perfectly acceptable to start talking to someone who you don't know. This is possibly the secret of Twitter's success!

1 **Read the Tweets again. Complete the definitions 1–5 with words from the box:**

DM	timeline	RT	@ replies	hashtag

1 In Twitter, the .... is the constantly updated list of Tweets from all the people you are following. The most recent Tweet appears at the top.

2 .... are replies sent publicly to a named Twitter user on the timeline. For example, if your friend @London_Cinema_Fan sends a Tweet about something that interests you, you could reply to them by starting your Tweet with @London_Cinema_Fan.

3 .... stands for 'Direct Message'. These are private messages which are only visible to you and the person you send them to. You can only send one to someone who is following you back.

4 .... stands for 'Retweet'. When you like what someone has Tweeted and you want to share it with your followers, you can click on the 'Retweet' button, or cut and paste their text into the 'What's happening' field and put 'RT' in front of it.

5 The .... (#) is an important concept on Twitter. Putting a # before a word or phrase means that other Twitter users can search for instances of that # in the timeline, e.g. if they are interested in a subject or are at a particular conference.

2 **Practise using some common Twitter conventions:**

1 Write an @reply to @Manchester_Music_Fan

2 Retweet one of the Tweets from the timeline.

3 Write a Tweet which contains a hashtag.

Looking more closely

1 **Read the Tweets 1–5 below. Complete them with hashtags from the box:**

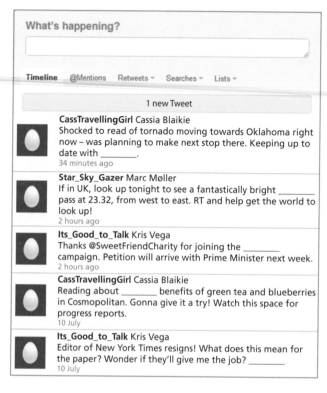

What's happening?

Timeline   @Mentions   Retweets ▾   Searches ▾   Lists ▾

1 new Tweet

CassTravellingGirl Cassia Blaikie
Shocked to read of tornado moving towards Oklahoma right now – was planning to make next stop there. Keeping up to date with _____.
34 minutes ago

Star_Sky_Gazer Marc Møller
If in UK, look up tonight to see a fantastically bright _____ pass at 23.32, from west to east. RT and help get the world to look up!
2 hours ago

Its_Good_to_Talk Kris Vega
Thanks @SweetFriendCharity for joining the _____ campaign. Petition will arrive with Prime Minister next week.
2 hours ago

CassTravellingGirl Cassia Blaikie
Reading about _____ benefits of green tea and blueberries in Cosmopolitan. Gonna give it a try! Watch this space for progress reports.
10 July

Its_Good_to_Talk Kris Vega
Editor of New York Times resigns! What does this mean for the paper? Wonder if they'll give me the job? _____
10 July

#endschoolbullying

#newspapers

#anti-ageing

#ISS

#CNNweather

Note: ISS = International Space Station

2 **Write an @reply to @Star_Sky_Gazer:**

- Retweet the first part of his message, including the hashtag.
- Make sure you include his Twitter name in the Retweet.
- Write a short comment of your own in square brackets after the Retweet.
- Remember not to go over 140 characters.

3 **Write an @reply to @Its_Good_to_Talk about the petition Tweet:**

- Remember to begin your Tweet with @Its_Good_to_Talk
- Ask a question about the Tweet.
- Say something supportive about the petition.

4 **Write an @reply to @CassTravellingGirl about the green tea and blueberries Tweet:**

- Include her Twitter name at the start.
- Give your opinion on what she has read.
- Make your Tweet sound friendly.

USEFUL TIPS

- When you write a Tweet, it must be under 140 characters (that's including spaces). Tweeting requires a special skill – the ability to write succinctly. If you have too many characters, think carefully about what you can delete without undermining the real meaning of what you want to say. Watch how other Tweeters stay within word count and copy what works best. Perhaps the units on texting and instant messaging (pages 8–11 and 12–15 could help you too).

- If your tweet is longer than 140 characters, don't just Tweet it and keep writing, as some people do. This will create a piece of text that is broken across two or more Tweets. It looks sloppy and ignores the whole point of Tweeting.

- If someone shares an interesting link or idea in a tweet and you want to use it in a new Tweet or share it with your followers, make sure you mention the original Tweeter in your Tweet. This is polite and is a common convention on Twitter.

- Remember that what you say on Twitter is public. If you are having a bad day, it can be tempting to Tweet about it to get some sympathy or reaction, but think carefully about who might be reading. Would you want your family or employer to read your Tweet? If not, don't Tweet it!

- One thing that really annoys other Twitter users is when one person dominates their timeline. Space out your Tweets and resist the temptation to Tweet everything that's on your mind. As the saying goes: less is often more.

Get writing

If you have not already done so, but would like to, then set up a Twitter account now. Follow these instructions to start making the most of your Twitter experience:

1 If you feel comfortable, use a real picture of yourself and your real name. This inspires trust in other people. Fill in your biography with some interesting information about yourself and your interests. People rarely respond if they don't know anything about who you are.

2 Follow at least 10–20 people. If you have friends on Twitter, follow them first. See who they are following and follow anyone who looks interesting. Next, follow some celebrities or public figures that you admire. Use the search field to find them. Finally, enter some search terms to do with your local area and subjects that interest you. Follow some random people that you find through these searches.

3 Now, read the Tweets in your timeline. Find some that interest you and send @replies to these people. Try to respond naturally, as though you were striking up a conversation with someone you had just met.

4 Keep going until you get into some conversations. Well done – you've begun your Twitter adventure!

19 REVIEWING ONLINE

BEFORE YOU START

Have you ever had a really good meal and wanted to tell people about it? We no longer just tell friends and family how our holiday went; we can write about it and publish our experiences online. When we buy goods online, we can review them to help other consumers make their choices. When you buy something through a website, you are likely to receive an email asking you to review your experience or purchase. Your opinion counts as much as anyone's, so get writing!

Understanding

Read the hotel review below. Would you stay at this hotel? Why?

| Home | Stockholm ▾ | Hotels | Flights | Holiday Rentals | Restaurants | Things to Do | Best of 2011 | More ▾ | Write a Review |

Waterview Inn, Boston, MA

'Great location and great price too!'

Reviewed 14 April 2012 by TwosCompany

My girlfriend and I hadn't stayed in Boston before and were recommended the Waterview Inn by a friend who told us he had always had great service there. Our room was clean, comfortable and good value for money. When we arrived, we were initially disappointed by the size of the room until we opened the curtains to a fantastic view across the harbour, which we would have happily paid a lot more money for!

The hotel is ideally located for sightseeing around Boston. It is next to the Metro, very close to Quincy Market, and the Freedom Trail starts nearby too.

Staff at the hotel were kind, helpful and happy, and because it was quite a small place we felt that we were getting personal service. We'd definitely stay there again.

Value ***   Rooms ****
Location ****   Cleanliness ****
Sleep Quality***   Service ****

Looking more closely

1 **Read the hotel review again. What do the phrases 1–6 mean?**

1 recommended

2 great service

3 good value for money

4 initially disappointed

5 ideally located

6 personal service

> For more typical phrases that might be helpful to you when writing an online review, see Unit 20.

2 **Do these words/phrases 1–10 describe a product, a service, or both?**

1 professional	6 disappointing
2 personal	7 poorly constructed
3 high quality	8 damaged
4 excellent	9 beautifully crafted
5 well made	10 exemplary

Language focus

Reviews are an expression of our opinions about a service or product. The following phrases are useful for writing reviews:

General:

I found/felt that …

I have used [product/service] for [length of time] …

In my opinion, …

Negative:

I was disappointed by …

I felt let down by …

I would not recommend [product/service] because …

Positive:

I'm really delighted by …

I would recommend [product/service] without hesitation.

I was extremely impressed by …

Read the review below. What is being reviewed? Is the review favourable?

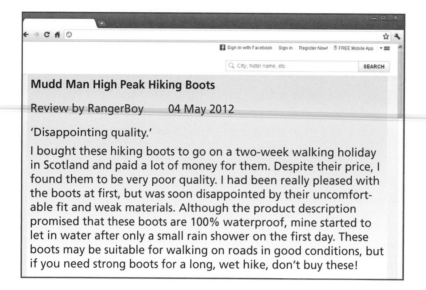

Mudd Man High Peak Hiking Boots

Review by RangerBoy   04 May 2012

'Disappointing quality.'

I bought these hiking boots to go on a two-week walking holiday in Scotland and paid a lot of money for them. Despite their price, I found them to be very poor quality. I had been really pleased with the boots at first, but was soon disappointed by their uncomfortable fit and weak materials. Although the product description promised that these boots are 100% waterproof, mine started to let in water after only a small rain shower on the first day. These boots may be suitable for walking on roads in good conditions, but if you need strong boots for a long, wet hike, don't buy these!

Writing appropriately

Read the following review. What is wrong with it?

"I can honestly say that I have never been so disgusted by a restaurant in my entire life. The Crazy Crayfish Cantina is quite simply the most ghastly place I've ever had the misfortune to eat at. Be warned!"

Reviews should be like reports, rather than stories. Long reviews full of descriptive passages and opinions can be amusing to read, but they aren't particularly helpful. It's important to stick to the facts when you write a review. If something was good, why was it good? If a service was poor, what exactly happened? By sticking to facts rather than opinions, you help your readers to make a proper judgment for themselves.

Reviews should be balanced. It is rare to buy a product or a service that is completely brilliant or totally awful – the experience is usually somewhere in between. If you had a bad meal in a restaurant perhaps the staff were friendly. If you bought a flatscreen TV with a great picture, perhaps the sound quality wasn't so good? Make sure your review tells the whole story.

A better version of the review would be more factual. For example:

"I was quite disgusted by the food at the Crazy Crayfish Cantina on the evening of Friday 6 July. My bowl of lobster bisque was cold and smelled 'off'. My companion's salad was wilted and the fries were undercooked. The staff were friendly enough, and replaced our dishes when asked, but I would not recommend this restaurant."

Get writing

1 **Online reviews often start with a single sentence which summarizes the whole review. Write one-line reviews for situations 1–3:**

1 You bought a really great kitchen appliance online.

2 You worked out in a really well-equipped gym with very unfriendly staff.

3 You bought a faulty radio and were refused a refund.

2 **Think about a product you have bought online (e.g. a book). Write a review of it.**

- Include the name of the book and its author.
- Include your name and the date.
- Write a one-line review that sums up your opinion.
- Write your review: What did you enjoy about the book? Did anything disappoint you?
- Even if you disliked the book in general, did you find anything enjoyable or pleasing about it? If so, mention that, even if it is a minor point, like an attractive cover.
- Would you recommend it to anyone else? If so, be specific about the type of person that might actually enjoy it.
- Write the last line of your review carefully. Sum up your thoughts in a similar way as you did at the beginning of your review.

USEFUL TIPS

- Before you write a review look to see what other people have written. If lots of people have already written reviews that reflect your opinion, perhaps you don't need to write anything else.
- Have you given the company a chance to fix the problem (e.g. by sending you a replacement or giving you a discount or apology)? If you tried to fix the problem, make sure you include the result in your review.
- Be polite and professional. If you are angry about a product or service, wait until you have calmed down before you write a review. Don't be rude or insulting. Readers will take a calm, sensible review much more seriously than an angry rant.
- Make sure you include all the important details. If it's a good review, tell readers how to get that product or service. If it's a bad review, tell them how to avoid the same situation.
- If the author has written several books, (or a company has produced many products you have used) it can be very helpful to compare it, for example 'I thought the storyline was much stronger in his last novel', or 'compared to the books he has previously written, the characters in this story are much more believable'. Telling people you have some experience of a book, or an item that you have bought, shows that you know what you are writing about and have some trustworthy experience to offer.

20 SELLING AND ADVERTISING ONLINE

BEFORE YOU START

Have you ever bought anything from an online auction site? Selling things online is becoming an increasingly popular way of making some extra cash or having a clearout before a moving house or travelling. Perhaps you've advertised online for something you need – maybe a new flatmate or help with your English. Selling and advertising online have their very own language choices with very specific abbreviations, vocabulary and 'advertising English'. It's helpful to be familiar with this new way of writing – you never know when you might need it!

Understanding

Read the following advert. What is being sold? Is it a 'bargain'?

Stylish three-piece suite: bargain!

£550, London

Three-piece suite for sale in excellent condition. Three-seater sofa plus two matching chairs and four cushions. Very attractive ruby-red cord fabric finish with gold stitching. Suite only six months old, carefully used, and has only minimal cosmetic wear. See detailed photo for small marks on back of sofa – these are hardly noticeable and will be rarely seen if the sofa is used against a wall.

Very comfortable, fashionable piece – sold reluctantly due to our move to a smaller house.

Originally purchased in Yearling Furniture for £1,100. Buy it now £550.
Pick up only.

✉: Reply to this add

Looking more closely

Read the advert again. What do these words and phrases mean?

1 excellent condition

2 three-seater

3 matching chairs

4 carefully used

5 minimal cosmetic wear.

6 sold reluctantly

Collocations

When we write adverts to sell items, there are many useful collocations we can use to describe what we are selling. A collocation is a set of words that commonly go together. For example, 'three-piece suite' is a collocation, as is 'excellent condition'.

Language focus

1 **Complete the collocations 1–5 with words from the box:**

1 excellent ....

2 good ....

3 original ....

4 good ....

5 .... condition

> immaculate
>
>   working order
>
> as new
>
>   packaging
>
>   condition

2 **Think of some collocations to simplify the sentences 1–4:**

Example   *The sofa has not been used much and still looks quite new.*

⇒ *The sofa is in* <u>*excellent condition*</u>.

1   I bought this phone 6 months ago and it is still in the same condition I bought it in.

2   The laptop comes in the same box as when I purchased it.

3   All the parts of the bike have been checked and are working fine.

4   For this price, the sofa would be an excellent purchase.

Abbreviations

You may notice some unfamiliar abbreviations on online auction sites like Ebay and 'classifieds' sites such as Gumtree. Here is a brief list of things you might see, and which might even be useful for your own adverts:

- BNWT: brand new with tags
- BNIB: brand new in box
- P&P: postage and packing
- RRP: retailer's recommended price
- GBP: Great Britain Pounds
- ASAP: as soon as possible
- 25yo: 25-year-old
- n/s: non smoker

Writing appropriately

Many collocations are formed with an adverb and an adjective.

Example   *The scratches on the phone are <u>hardly noticeable</u>.*

1 **Match the adverbs 1–5 and the adjectives a–e to make some common collocations:**

1	fully	**a**	used
2	barely	**b**	priced
3	beautifully	**c**	operational
4	fairly	**d**	situated
5	ideally	**e**	decorated

2 **Read the advert below. What kind of flatmate are the writers looking for?**

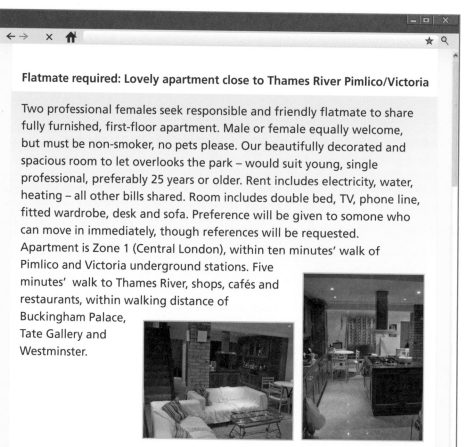

Flatmate required: Lovely apartment close to Thames River Pimlico/Victoria

Two professional females seek responsible and friendly flatmate to share fully furnished, first-floor apartment. Male or female equally welcome, but must be non-smoker, no pets please. Our beautifully decorated and spacious room to let overlooks the park – would suit young, single professional, preferably 25 years or older. Rent includes electricity, water, heating – all other bills shared. Room includes double bed, TV, phone line, fitted wardrobe, desk and sofa. Preference will be given to somone who can move in immediately, though references will be requested.
Apartment is Zone 1 (Central London), within ten minutes' walk of Pimlico and Victoria underground stations. Five minutes' walk to Thames River, shops, cafés and restaurants, within walking distance of Buckingham Palace, Tate Gallery and Westminster.

3 **Read the advert again. What do the collocations 1–6 mean?**

1 fully furnished

2 non-smoker

3 beautifully decorated

4 double bed

5 fitted wardrobe

6 within walking distance

Get writing

1 **Most adverts need a headline – a sentence that tells readers what you are selling and that makes it look appealing. Write headlines for the following items or services 1–3:**

1 Spanish classes with a very good Spanish teacher who has lots of experience.

2 A games console which is almost new and comes with lots of games

3 An old sofa which is good value for money but not in great condition.

USEFUL TIPS

- Adverts should be clear and informative. A good way to plan your advert is to imagine you are the buyer, rather than the seller. Ask yourself what information you would want to know in order to buy the item. Make a list of questions.
- Before you write your advert, look online to see if anyone else is selling something similar. How have they described it? What price have they set? You can use this information to help you write your own advert.
- Plan your advert before you write it. Organize similar information into paragraphs. For example, one paragraph to describe the item and another to explain how it should be paid for and collected.
- Be honest. If your item is damaged in some way, describe the problem and show photos if possible. Online selling sites generally have a rating system, and if you mis-sell an item (i.e. sell something that is different to how you describe it) your buyer will give you a bad rating

2 **Write an advert for an item you want to sell online. Answer these questions:**

- How old is the item?
- What condition is it in?
- What is included in the sale?
- Are there any special conditions (e.g. for collection)?

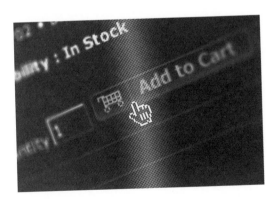

APPENDIX 1 – Useful phrases

1. Emails

Formal emails

Opening phrase	Closing phrase	Notes
Dear Sir / Madam *Dear Sir or Madam*	*Yours faithfully*	When you don't know the name of the person you are writing to.
Dear Mr / Mrs / Ms / Miss [Family name]	*Yours sincerely / Yours truly*	When you know the name of the person you are writing to but you have never met or you hardly know the person.
Dear [First name]	*Best regards / Kind regards*	When you know the person you are writing to well enough to use their first name.
Hi [First name]	*Best regards / Kind regards / All the best*	When you know the person you are writing to fairly well and have a friendly relationship with them.
[First name] / *[First name], hi*	*All the best / Cheers / Best / Thanks*	Some people dislike being addressed by just their first name in the opening line of an email. Nevertheless, this is becoming an acceptable way to open emails.

Informal emails

Opening phrase	Closing phrase	Notes
Hi (First name)	*All the best / Cheers / Best / Thanks*	
Hi / Hello / Yo	*Cheers / Bye / Speak soon / Later / Hugs / Kisses / (person's initial)*	There are many informal ways to open and close informal emails between friends. These are just a few.
(no opening phrase)	(no closing phrase)	In informal emails there may sometimes be no opening or closing phrase. This is especially common in a sequence of quick emails between two people who know each other well.

2. Invitations

Formal

Formal phrases for invitations

We request the pleasure of your company at ...
You are cordially invited to ...
We would be delighted if you could join us at ...
We ask you to be present at ...
We request the honour of your presence at ...

Formal phrases for accepting an invitation

We gladly accept your invitation.
We would be delighted to accept your invitation.
I am honoured to be invited and gratefully accept your invitation.

Formal phrases for declining an invitation

It is with great regret that I have to decline your generous invitation.
Sadly, we have to decline your invitation due to a prior engagement.
We would love to come to your event, but unfortunately we have already accepted another invitation on that date.

Informal

Informal phrases for invitations

Come and join us at ...
We'd love it if you could join us at / come to / come along to ...
We're having a party / getting married / getting engaged ...

Informal phrases for accepting an invitation

We'd love to come along.
Thanks for the invite / invitation. I'll be there!
Can't wait! Really looking forward to it!
See you there! / We'll be there!

Informal phrases for declining an invitation

Really sorry, but I've got something else on then. Another time!
Thanks so much for the invitation, but unfortunately I won't be able to make it.
Thanks, but we've got other plans then.

3. Expressing reactions

Thanks

Thank you very / so much.
We are so / very grateful …
I can't tell you how grateful we are for …
I'm so grateful for your gift / so grateful that you could come …
Many / Profound thanks.
With thanks.
Thanks so much for …
I can't thank you enough for …
Thank you very much for your … You are too generous!
Thank you very, very much for your very generous gift of …
I can't express what it means to me that you could come …
Thanks again for your lovely gift / coming to our party …
Thank you for thinking of us!

Pleasure

I'm so delighted with / by …
I can't tell you how delighted I was / am by …
What a great pleasure it was to …
It was a great pleasure to see you …
We were absolutely delighted by …

Surprise

I couldn't believe it when …
What you did was so lovely / amazing / incredible …
It was such a lovely surprise when …
I can hardly believe what you did!
What a lovely / amazing surprise …

Admiration

What you did was so wonderful.
Your gift was so beautifully made / such an exquisite piece of work …
You worked so hard and I really appreciate it.
What a wonderful idea!
I'm so impressed by what you did.

4. Polite enquiries

I wonder if you could …?
I wonder if you would mind …?
Please could you …?
Could you possibly …?
Would you mind telling me …?
Would it be possible (for you) to …?
I would like to enquire whether / if …?
If you don't / wouldn't mind …?
I was wondering whether / if it would be possible to …?
If it's not too much trouble …?

5. Confirming arrangements

Can I just check / confirm that …?
Could you confirm that …?
Just to confirm, … [+ details of what you think has been confirmed]?
As discussed / agreed, …
…. Is that correct?
Am I right / correct in thinking that …?
Could we just go over that again?
Can you repeat that so I know what we've agreed?
Could you remind me what we discussed / agreed?
Let's just go over that again?
Could you repeat / go over / explain that once more?
Just to be sure, could we confirm that …?

6. Justifying a decision

I've [made X decision] because …
Because of [factors X, Y and Z] I've decided that …
X is better because …
If we do X, then Y will happen.
I realise X is more expensive / less convenient than we discussed, but …
I know X is more expensive / less convenient than Y, but …
Not only is X cheaper / better / more interesting, but …
'That way …' (a useful phrase for starting an explanation about why something is a good idea)
I know this sounds like a crazy / strange / bad idea, but …
Let me explain why I made this decision …

7. Complaining

Phrases to show that you are normally used to better service

Until recently, I have enjoyed …

… has always been excellent. Recently however, …

I was surprised to experience …

Despite being used to excellent service, recently I have experienced …

Although I am usually impressed by …

Because [service / product] has an excellent reputation I was very surprised / disappointed by …

I am used to a much higher standard of service / quality of product than this.

As a regular customer I was shocked / upset / surprised by …

Phrases to express disappointment

I was extremely / deeply disappointed to / by …

I am very / extremely / deeply disappointed in …

I expect a much higher standard of service from …

I am upset / surprised about …

I am not at all happy about …

This level of service / quality of product is simply unacceptable.

I am not prepared to accept this level of service / quality of product.

Phrases to ask for a resolution to a problem

Unless (X happens), I (will / won't do X).

Because of X, I expect you to …

Due to X, I ask you / request that …

I expect / demand a swift resolution to this problem.

I would like an apology / explanation / discount / refund.

I would like you to contact me.

I expect you to resolve this matter by [date / time].

8. Writing reviews

General

I found / felt that …
I have used [product / service] for [length of time] …
In my opinion, …
It is my opinion that …
IMO (= In my opinion) …
IMHO (= In my humble opinion) …
There is no question in my mind that …
Let me tell you about …
Let me explain / describe …

Negative

I was disappointed by …
I felt let down by …
I would not recommend [product / service] because …
Steer clear!
Stay well away from this!
To be avoided at all costs.
Don't waste your money on this.

Positive

I'm really delighted by …
I would recommend [product / service] without hesitation.
I wouldn't hesitate to recommend …
I was extremely impressed by …
You really have to try … It's fabulous / amazing / brilliant / excellent!
Just excellent!
Try it for yourself – you won't be disappointed!
Money well spent!
Top / Full marks!
10/10 (ten out of ten = full marks).

APPENDIX 2 – Sentence structure

1. Sentence parts

1.1 Subject, verb, object

The basic English sentence contains a subject, a verb and an object.

Kasper loves writing.

In this sentence 'Kasper' is the subject, 'loves' is the verb and 'writing' is the object.

1.2 Phrases

A phrase is a group of words that work together in a sentence to give more information.

*We stared at **the angry woman**.* (noun phrase)

*She patted the dog **on its head**.* (prepositional phrase)

1.3 Clauses

There are four main types of clause:

Main clause	Contains a subject and verb and may stand alone as a simple sentence.
Dependent (or subordinate) clause	Contains a subordinate conjunction, a noun and a verb, and cannot stand alone as a complete sentence. It is dependent on a main clause to express a complete idea.
Relative clause	Begins with a relative pronoun and also contains a noun or a verb. Sometimes a clause like this contains only a relative pronoun and a verb e.g. 'who left'.
Noun clause	Functions like a single noun e.g. *Lunch* (noun) *was fantastic.* *What we ate at lunchtime* (noun clause) *was fantastic.*

Main clauses and dependent clauses

A dependent (or subordinate) clause adds information to a main clause. It starts with a subordinating conjunction or a relative pronoun. Although it contains a subject and a verb, a dependent clause cannot stand alone as a sentence.

Main clause	Dependent clause
Jonas was nervous about their first date	*because he had met Eleni only once before.*

Relative clauses

When dependent clauses begin with a relative pronoun (e.g. *that, which, who* etc.), they are called relative clauses. Again, they cannot stand alone as sentences, because they do not express complete ideas.

Main clause	Relative clause
Rachel recognized the young man	*who was eating chips from a brown paper bag.*

2. Sentence functions

2.1 Statements

A statement (also known as a declarative) gives factual information or an opinion. For example:

I saw Jonah yesterday.

That film was brilliant!

Josh said he didn't want to come to the party this evening.

2.2 Questions

A question (also known as an interrogative) must be followed by a question mark. It can be a direct question (i.e. something we ask in order to get an answer) or a rhetorical question (a general question to which an answer is not expected).

What time does French class start? (direct question)

I wonder what I'll have for lunch? (rhetorical question)

2.3 Commands

Commands (also known as imperatives) are instructions we give to other people.

Pass me the salad.

I need you to come home at once!

---

3. Sentence types

3.1 Simple sentences

A simple sentence contains at least a subject and a verb. It is an independent clause and expresses a complete idea.

I like to watch TV in the evenings.

3.2 Compound sentences

A compound sentence is made up of two independent clauses linked by a conjunction.

It's Christmas Day, and I'm having a lovely time with my family.

3.3 Complex sentences

A complex sentence contains an independent clause with one or more dependent clauses linked to it.

Because of the weather, which was awful, I decided to stay indoors.

3.4 Compound-complex sentences

A compound-complex sentence contains one or more independent clauses with at least one dependent clause.

Tim saw Jules walking down the street, and because she looked so sad, he stopped her and asked what was wrong.

APPENDIX 3 – Discourse markers

Discourse markers

In writing, discourse markers are words that help us link ideas together (which is why they are sometimes called linking words). They help our readers to make sense of what we are writing.

There are lots of discourse markers for you to choose from, but it is important not to overuse them in writing or your work will sound too formal. Read some extended articles in good quality newspapers or some examples of good academic essays so that you can see how discourse markers should be used.

Adding another related point

moreover	John's behaviour at school recently has been unacceptable. Moreover, his exam results have been very poor.
in addition	Part-time English classes are offered. In addition we run classes in word-processing and computing.
furthermore	Let's go inside. It's nearly dark and furthermore, it's going to rain.
also	She is a brilliant writer. Also, she is gorgeous.

Presenting a contrasting idea

| however | Most of the class failed the exam. However, a couple of students did very well. |
| on the other hand | Prices of foods and consumer goods fell. Wages on the other hand increased. |

Presenting a surprising or unexpected contrasting idea

even though	Even though I'm working alone, there are people I can ask for help or advice.
despite	Despite a bad choice of school, Elaine got enough qualifications to go to university.
although	Their system worked, although no one was sure how.
in spite of	He hired her in spite of the fact that she had never sung on stage.

Showing what the result of something is

therefore	The process is much quicker and therefore cheaper.
consequently	They have been studying continuously since September, and are consequently tired and unhappy.
as a result	Large numbers of fish are dying as a result of pollution in the oceans.
for this reason	The driver was trapped in his vehicle. For this reason, the fire service was called.
because of this	Many families are worried about debt. Because of this we offer free independent financial advice at the centre.

Demonstrating why something has happened / is true

because	Maybe they won because they had the best players?
since	I'm forever on a diet, since I put on weight easily.
as	Lighting is important as it creates warmth in a room.

APPENDIX 4 – Punctuation

1. Punctuation

(1) full stop; (US: period) .

- Use it to show where a sentence ends. Note: all sentences must begin with a capital letter.
  You're good at writing.

(2) comma ,

- Use it to divide items in lists, where it could be replaced by 'and' or 'or'. It's not necessary before the final 'and'.
  Please buy bread, milk, butter and cheese.
- Use it in a list of adjectives where an 'and' would also be appropriate.
  It was a bright, sunny, crisp autumn day.
- Use it when two independent clauses (or simple sentences) are joined together by a conjunction.
  She studied all year, yet she failed the exam.
- Use it after a conjunctive adverb (moreover, nevertheless, etc.) following a semicolon.
  They searched for hours; however, they couldn't find her ring.
- Use it to set off interjections (words or phrases that express an emotion).
  'I've eaten, honey.'
  'Goodness, it's late.'
- Use it to separate parts of a sentence that contain 'supplementary' information.
  Every chocolate, and there were many, was as good as the last.
- Use it to separate a dependent clause from an independent clause.
  If it keeps raining, we will have to cancel our picnic.
- No comma is needed if the dependent clause comes *after* the independent one.
  We will have to cancel our picnic if it keeps raining.

(3) question mark ?

- Use it to show a direct question.
  What's your name?
- When the question is indirect, no question mark is needed.
  She wondered where the road went.

> Note: See p33 for question marks when making polite enquiries.

(4) exclamation mark !

- Use it to show that information is important, exciting or surprising.
  Danger!
- If at all possible, avoid using it in formal or professional writing.

(5) apostrophe '

- Use it to show a contracted word.
  That's my hat.
- Use it to show possession.
  Simon's essay was the best.
  It was Ladies' Day at Ascot.
- Use it to show time or quantity.
  One week's holiday. In three days' time.
- Use it to show a shortened date.
  He was from the class of '96.

(6) single quotation marks ' ... '

- Use these to highlight a particular word or short phrase in a sentence.
  She had put a comma before the final 'and'.
- In British English we normally use these to indicate quoted speech or text.
  The politician said he was 'deeply sorry' for what had happened.

(7) double quotation marks " ... "

- In British English we normally use these to mark off a quotation within quoted speech or text.
  The politician said, 'I have apologized to my wife, who, in her own words, said "nothing will come between us." I am lucky to have her by my side.'

(8) colon :

- Use it to introduce a part of a sentence that dramatically explains, undermines, or balances the first. The colon can act as a silent 'that is', or 'because'.
  There is only one thing I need: pizza.
  He couldn't stop shaking: he had terrible stage-fright.
- Use it to introduce a list after a complete sentence.
  There are three things you need for a good holiday: cash, enthusiasm and a few plans.
- Use it to introduce examples.
  Scientists have found the following techniques to be of use: ...

(9) semi-colon ;

- Use it to join two independent clauses (or simple sentences) instead of a comma and conjunction.
  He knew everything about me; I knew nothing about him.
- Use it before conjunctive adverbs like 'nevertheless', 'moreover' and 'however'.
  He had left her forever; however, she had never been happier.
- Use it to make sense in a list when you have lots of commas.
  The University welcomes some distinguished guests: Professor Ralph, Chancellor, Tutor, and Dean of Studies at The University of Stern; Prof. Farish, Tutor in English, French and Armenian Studies, Mahler University; and Mr Borge, writer critic, and observer of Higher Education.

(10) brackets/parantheses ( )

- Use them to add extra information that is relevant but isn't as important as the main information in the sentence.
  Sam was very excited about the flight (he had never flown before).

- Use them to add your own comments as writer of the text.
  This superstar (who only spoke to me reluctantly) seemed to be a very private man.

- Square brackets can be used to explain the grammar or meaning of a direct quote without changing the quote itself.
  'He [David Crystal] is a prolific and authoritative writer on the subject of language.'

(11) hyphen -

- Use it when a descriptive compound (e.g. sixth-form) comes before a noun (but not normally after it).
  The sixth-form pupils will take their exams in the main hall.

- Use it to prevent confusion where a word could be misread, or where a descriptive phrase could be misunderstood.
  He re-signed the contract because his first signature was illegible.
  There were twenty-odd people at the staff party.
  There was a long-forgotten scarf lying by the road.

- Use it to write out numbers
  My twenty-fifth birthday.

- Use it to make pronunciation clear when consonants or vowels appear next to each other.
  The ornament had a shell-like shape.

- Use it after a prefix that is followed by a name or date.
  His politics had been pro-Thatcher, but that was pre-1990.

- Use it to show a common second element in a list.
  They bought first- and second-class stamps.

(12) dash –

- Use it to create a break from the previous text for emphasis.
  I won't eat meat – I never will.

- Use it where you might also use paired commas or brackets, but you want the interruption to be more definite or 'louder'.
  He lost his thesis – every last page of it – in the house fire.

(13) ellipsis …

- Use it to leave a sentence unfinished with an implicit suggestion. It is usually limited to either dramatic, or very informal, writing.
  We may not have a job vacancy for you now, but if you were to check again in two weeks …

- Use it to indicate that words have been omitted from quoted text, or that some words were lost or illegible in an original manuscript.
  The crew were missing for six long days and … finally found by a scout helicopter on Sunday 25th August.

(14) forward slash /

- Use it to show two or more options. You can safely use it where 'or' would also work.
  Coffee/tea will be served at 2 o'clock.

- It is also used in some abbreviations.
  Don't go w/out me.

APPENDIX 5 – Short forms

Emoticons for texting and instant messaging

☺	smiling / happy
☹	sad / unhappy
;)	joking / don't take this seriously
:D	big grin / happy
<3	heart / love
\o/	excitement / jumping for joy
:0	surprise / shocked face
</3	broken heart / no love
d(^_^)b	headphones / listening to music
(^_-)	winking
o/ \o	high five
:-P	sticking your tongue out at someone (cheeky, rather than rude)
:X	'my lips are sealed' (= 'I'm not telling you anything.')
@}-;--	rose / romantic

Symbols for notes

&	and
+	plus
=	equals / is the same as
≠	does not equal / is different from / is not the same as
>	is greater than / more than
<	is less than
"	repeat the text that you see above
@	at
→	connects two points
←	relates back to a previous point
?	uncertain / not sure about this point
↑	increasing
↓	decreasing
∴	therefore
#	number
$	dollars / money

Shorthand   (These shorthand abbreviations can be used in emails to people you know.)

abt.	about
b/c	because

c.	circa (meaning 'around the time')	
cf.	compare	
ch.	chapter	
D.O.B.	date of birth	
e.g.	for example	
esp.	especially	
etc.	and all the rest	
govt.	government	
i.e.	that is / in other words	
max.	maximum	
min.	minimum	
mth.	month	
no./nos.	number / numbers	
N.B.	important	
p./pp.	page / pages	
re.	concerning	
sbd.	somebody	
sth.	something	
vs.	versus (meaning 'against')	
w/	with	
w/o	without	
yr.	year	

Note: not everyone uses a full stop after a shortened word like 'sbd.'. It is up to you whether to use a full stop or not, but if you do, make sure you use it consistently.

Twitter conventions

RT	= retweet	Use in front of another person's tweet that you want to share with your followers.
MT	= modified tweet	Use when you have shortened someone else's tweet in order to retweet it. Try never to change the meaning of someone else's tweet – this is a real Twitter no-no!
DM	= direct message	Use to send private messages to people that you follow, who also follow you.
@	= at replies	Put in front of the Twitter name of the person you want to send a message to. Note that this will appear in the public timeline, so don't use it for private or sensitive information.
#	= hashtag	Use to allow readers to search for tweets about specific subjects. For example, if you are at a conference, find the conference hashtag and add this to all your tweets connected with that conference.
[...]	= square brackets	Use when you want to insert a comment of your own next to a retweet. This helps your reader to distinguish the original tweet from your comment. Regular parentheses (round brackets) are also acceptable.
#FF	= Follow Friday	For recommending people to follow. Use on Fridays alongside the Twitter name(s) of the people you are recommending. A short explanation of who they are and why they are worth following is also helpful.

APPENDIX 6 – Proofreading: what to do after you finish writing

How to proofread

When you have finished writing a piece of text, you should always proofread it thoroughly. This means reading your text very closely to check that it reads well, it is free of errors, factual mistakes and inconsistency.

Step-by-step procedures for proofreading:

- Print out your text and be prepared to mark up the paper printout in a noticeably coloured pen.
- Read your text, concentrating on one type of error at a time. Start, for example, by checking your paragraphing and sentence structure. Then start at the beginning again to check your word choice and spelling. Don't trust your judgement if you are unsure – use a dictionary. Then go back and ensure that your punctuation is correct and consistent throughout the text.
- No matter how many times you have done so, double-check names, dates numbers and quotes to ensure they are all correctly spelled, listed, factually correct and correctly attributed.
- Check that your typography is consistent – check for unintended changes in font. Check that all your headers, titles, captions and footnotes are in the correct style, size and font (or in the pattern that you have decided on).
- Check line spacing and ensure that it is consistent.
- Make your revisions on screen from your marked-up paper proof.

Tips for proofreading:

- Most importantly, clear your desk of all other papers and reading material.
- Always proofread from a paper printout, not from a computer screen.
- Proofread in a silent room.
- Don't proofread when you are tired or when you have been working on the document for a long time. If possible, look at it the next day.
- Don't hurry!
- When you think your document is clear of all errors, give it to someone else to proofread. You will be surprised what a 'fresh pair of eyes' will see.
- Do not rely on your PC's spellchecker. Your text may be spellchecked into a word you did not want to use – which can be very bad on a CV or in an academic essay.
- Actually say out loud the words that you are reading; this helps you focus on the letters in front of you and makes spelling mistakes easier to find.
- Be careful of line ends: watch out for missing full stops, and for words appearing at a line end that also appear at the beginning of the next line.
- Make sure that the decisions you make are standard throughout a text – don't change your mind halfway through.
- Lastly, read your finished, corrected text out loud again. If your voice falters or you get out of breath, it's likely that your punctuation needs some attention.

MINI-DICTIONARY

Some of the most difficult words from each unit are defined here in this Mini-dictionary. The definitions are extracts from the *Collins COBUILD Advanced Dictionary* and focus on the meanings of the words in the contexts in which they appear in the book.

Unit 1

cheer up (cheers up, cheering up, cheered up) PHRASAL VERB When you **cheer up** or when something **cheers** you **up**, you stop feeling depressed and become more cheerful. • *I think he misses her terribly. You might cheer him up.*

ability N-SING Your **ability to** do something is the fact that you can do it. • *He has the ability to bring out the best in others.*

permission N-UNCOUNT If someone who has authority over you gives you **permission to** do something, they say that they will allow you to do it. • *He asked permission to leave the room.*

obligation (obligations) N-VAR If you have an **obligation to** do something, it is your duty to do that thing. • *When teachers assign homework, students usually feel an obligation to do it.*

scenario (scenarios) N-COUNT If you talk about a likely or possible **scenario**, you are talking about the way in which a situation may develop. • *Try to imagine all the possible scenarios and what action you would take.*

informative ADJ Something that is **informative** gives you useful information. • *The adverts are not very informative.*

expression (expressions) N-VAR Your **expression** is the way that your face looks at a particular moment. It shows what you are thinking or feeling. • *Levin sat there, an expression of sadness on his face.*

Unit 2

time-consuming ADJ If something is **time-consuming**, it takes a lot of time. • *It's just very time consuming to get such a large quantity of data.*

congratulate (congratulates, congratulating, congratulated) VERB If you **congratulate** someone, you praise them for something good that they have done. • *We specifically wanted to congratulate certain players.*

achievement (achievements) N-COUNT An **achievement** is something which someone has succeeded in doing, especially after a lot of effort. • *Reaching this agreement so quickly was a great achievement.*

technique (techniques) N-COUNT A **technique** is a particular method of doing an activity, usually a method that involves practical skills. • *...tests performed using a new technique.*

skip (skips, skipping, skipped) VERB If you **skip** something that you usually do or something that you planned to do, you decide not to do it. • *It is important not to skip meals.*

acronym (acronyms) N-COUNT An **acronym** is a word composed of the first letters of the words in a phrase, especially when this is used as a name. An example of an acronym is NATO which is made up of the first letters of the 'North Atlantic Treaty Organization'.

abbreviation (abbreviations) N-COUNT An **abbreviation** is a short form of a word or phrase, made by leaving out some of the letters or by using only the first letter of each word. • *The postal abbreviation for Kansas is KS.*

Unit 3

on the move PHRASE If you are **on the move**, you are going from one place to another. • *Jack never wanted to stay in one place for very long, so they were always on the move.*

resume (resumes, resuming, resumed) VERB If you **resume** an activity or if it **resumes**, it begins again. [FORMAL] • *After the war he resumed his duties at Emmanuel College.*

butt in (butts in, butting in, butted in) PHRASAL VERB If you say that someone **is butting in**, you are criticizing the fact that they are joining in a conversation or activity without being asked to. [DISAPPROVAL] • *'I should think not,' Sarah butted in.*

tone (tones) N-COUNT Someone's **tone** is a quality in their voice which shows what they are feeling or thinking. • *I still didn't like his tone of voice.*

disappointment N-UNCOUNT **Disappointment** is the state of feeling disappointed. • *Book early to avoid disappointment.*

annoying ADJ Someone or something that is **annoying** makes you feel fairly angry and impatient. • *The annoying thing about the scheme is that it's confusing.*

prompt (prompts) N-COUNT A **prompt** is a word, phrase, or gesture that helps or encourages someone to continue when they stop speaking. • *She was saved by a prompt from one of her hosts.*

Unit 4

traditional ADJ **Traditional** customs, beliefs, or methods are ones that have existed for a long time without changing. • *...traditional teaching methods.*

old-fashioned ADJ **Old-fashioned** ideas, customs, or values are the ideas, customs, and values of the past. • *She has some old-fashioned values and can be very strict.*

invite (invites, inviting, invited) **1.** VERB If you **invite** someone to something such as a party or a meal, you ask them to come to it. • *She invited him to her 26th birthday party in New Jersey.* **2.** N-COUNT An **invite** is an invitation to something such as a party or a meal. [INFORMAL] • *They haven't got an invite to the wedding.*

customary ADJ **Customary** is used to describe things that people usually do in a particular society or in particular circumstances. [FORMAL] • *It is customary to offer a drink or a snack to guests.*

omit (omits, omitting, omitted) VERB If you **omit** something, you do not include it in an activity or piece of work, deliberately or accidentally. • *Our apologies to David Pannick for omitting his name from last week's article.*

precise ADJ Something that is **precise** is exact and accurate in all its details. • *He does not talk too much and what he has to say is precise and to the point.*

emotional ADJ **Emotional** means concerned with emotions and feelings. • *The ceremony was a highly emotional occasion for all of us.*

Unit 5

unnecessary ADJ If you describe something as **unnecessary**, you mean that it is not needed or does not have to be done, and is undesirable. • *He accused Diana of making an unnecessary fuss.*

in addition PHRASE You use **in addition** when you want to mention another item connected with the subject you are discussing. • *There's a postage and packing fee in addition to the repair charge.*

typical ADJ You use **typical** to describe someone or something that shows the most usual characteristics of a particular type of person or thing, and is therefore a good example of that type. • *Cheney is everyone's image of a typical cop: a big white guy, six foot, 220 pounds.*

talented ADJ Someone who is **talented** has a natural ability to do something well. • *Howard is a talented pianist.*

reaction (reactions) N-VAR Your **reaction** to something that has happened or something that you have experienced is what you feel, say, or do because of it. • *He was surprised that his answer should have caused such a strong reaction.*

identify (identifies, identifying, identified) VERB If you **identify** something, you discover or notice its existence. • *Having identified the problem, the question arises of how to overcome it.*

sincere ADJ If you say that someone is **sincere**, you approve of them because they really mean the things they say. You can also describe someone's behaviour and beliefs as **sincere**. • *He accepted her apologies as sincere.*

Unit 6

shorten (shortens, shortening, shortened) VERB If you **shorten** an object or if it **shortens**, it becomes smaller in length. • *Her father paid £1,000 for an operation to shorten her nose.*

miss out (misses out, missing out, missed out) PHRASAL VERB If you **miss out** something or someone, you fail to include them. • *There should be an apostrophe here, and look, you've missed out the word 'men' altogether!*

snapshot (snapshots) **1.** N-COUNT A **snapshot** is a photograph that is taken quickly and casually. **2.** N-COUNT If something provides you with a **snapshot of** a place or situation, it gives you a brief idea of what that place or situation is like. • *The interviews present a remarkable snapshot of Britain in those dark days.*

chilly (chillier, chilliest) ADJ Something that is **chilly** is unpleasantly cold. • *It was a chilly afternoon.*

lobster (lobsters) **1.** N-VAR A **lobster** is a sea creature that has a hard shell, two large claws, and eight legs. • *She sold me a couple of live lobsters.* **2.** N-UNCOUNT **Lobster** is the flesh of a lobster eaten as food. • *...lobster on a bed of fresh vegetables.*

cable car (cable cars) N-COUNT A **cable car** is a vehicle for taking people up mountains or steep hills. It is pulled by a moving cable.

mention (mentions, mentioning, mentioned) VERB If you **mention** something, you say something about it, usually briefly. • *She did not mention her mother's absence.*

Unit 7

uncomplicated ADJ If you describe someone or something as **uncomplicated**, you approve of them because they are easy to deal with or understand. • *...good, fresh British cooking with its uncomplicated, direct flavours.*

puzzle (puzzles, puzzling, puzzled) VERB If something **puzzles** you, you do not understand it and feel confused. • *My sister puzzles me and causes me anxiety.* **puz|zling** ADJ • *His letter poses a number of puzzling questions.*

utility room (utility rooms) N-COUNT A **utility room** is a room in a house which is usually connected to the kitchen and which contains things such as a washing machine, sink, and cleaning equipment.

emergency (emergencies) N-COUNT An **emergency** is an unexpected and difficult or dangerous situation, especially an accident, which happens suddenly and which requires quick action to deal with it. • *He deals with emergencies promptly.*

expense (expenses) N-VAR **Expense** is the money that something costs you or that you need to spend in order to do something. • *It was not a fortune but would help to cover household expenses.*

category (categories) N-COUNT If people or things are divided into **categories**, they are divided into groups in such a way that the members of each group are similar to each other in some way. • *The tables were organised into six different categories.*

contact ADJ Your **contact** details or number are information such as a telephone number where you can be contacted. • *You must leave your full name and contact details when you phone.*

qualities, or approve of what they have done. • *You can do no harm by paying a woman compliments.*

flexible ADJ Something or someone that is **flexible** is able to change easily and adapt to different conditions and circumstances as they occur. • *Look for software that's flexible enough for a range of abilities.*

idea N-SING If someone gives you an **idea of** something, they give you information about it without being very exact or giving a lot of detail. • *Could you give us an idea of the range of complaints you've been receiving?*

contract (contracts, contracting, contracted) VERB When something **contracts** or when something **contracts** it, it becomes smaller or shorter. • *New research shows that an excess of meat and salt can contract muscles.*

tuxedo (tuxedos) N-COUNT A **tuxedo** is a black or white jacket worn by men for formal social events. [mainly AM - in BRIT, usually use **dinner jacket**]

slang N-UNCOUNT **Slang** consists of words, expressions, and meanings that are informal and are used by people who know each other very well or who have the same interests. • *Archie liked to think he kept up with current slang.*

Unit 9

clarity N-UNCOUNT The **clarity** of something such as a book or argument is its quality of being well explained and easy to understand. • *...the ease and clarity with which the author explains difficult technical and scientific subjects.*

break up (breaks up, breaking up, broke up, broken up) PHRASAL VERB When something **breaks up** or when you **break** it **up**, it separates or is divided into several smaller parts. • *Break up the chocolate and melt it.*

interchangeably ADV Things that can be used **interchangeably** can be exchanged with each other without it making any difference. • *These expressions are often used interchangeably, but they do have different meanings.*

secure (secures, securing, secured) VERB If you **secure** an object, you fasten it firmly to another object. • *The frames are secured by horizontal rails to the back wall.*

assemble (assembles, assembling, assembled) VERB To **assemble** something means to collect it together or to fit the different parts of it together. • *She had been trying to assemble the bomb when it went off in her arms.*

separate (separates, separating, separated) VERB If you **separate** people or things that are together, or if they **separate**, they move apart. • *Police moved in to separate the two groups.*

obstacle (obstacles) N-COUNT An **obstacle** is an object that makes it difficult for you to go where you want to go, because it is in your way. • *Most competition cars will only roll over if they hit an obstacle.*

Unit 10

repetition (repetitions) N-VAR **Repetition** means using the same words again. • *He could also have cut out much of the repetition and thus saved many pages.*

transfer (transfers) N-VAR A **transfer** is the movement of something or someone **from** one place **to** another. • *The bank reserves the right to reverse any transfers or payments.*

disagreement (disagreements) N-VAR When there is **disagreement** about something, people disagree or argue about what should be done. • *My instructor and I had a brief disagreement.*

Unit 8

upset (upsets, upsetting, upset) VERB If something **upsets** you, it makes you feel worried or unhappy. • *She warned me not to say anything to upset him.*

compliment (compliments) N-COUNT A **compliment** is a polite remark that you say to someone to show that you like their appearance, appreciate their

guarantee (guarantees, guaranteeing, guaranteed) VERB If you **guarantee** something, you promise that it will definitely happen, or that you will do or provide it for someone. • *All students are guaranteed campus accommodation for their first year.*

people carrier (people carriers) N-COUNT A **people carrier** is a large family car which looks similar to a van and has three rows of seats for passengers.

evidence (evidences) N-UNCOUNT **Evidence** is anything that you see, experience, read, or are told that causes you to believe that something is true or has really happened. • *To date there is no evidence to support this theory.*

allergic ADJ If you are **allergic to** something, you become ill or get a rash when you eat it, smell it, or touch it. • *I'm allergic to cats.*

Unit 11

downturn (downturns) N-COUNT If there is a **downturn** in the economy or in a company or industry, it becomes worse or less successful than it had been. • *...unchanged profits for 1990 due to a sharp downturn in the industry.*

unavoidable ADJ If something is **unavoidable**, it cannot be avoided or prevented. • *Managers said the job losses were unavoidable.*

morale N-UNCOUNT **Morale** is the amount of confidence and cheerfulness that a group of people have. • *Many pilots are suffering from low morale.*

collectability N-UNCOUNT The **collectability** of an object is how highly it is valued by collectors because it is rare or beautiful. • *A camera's date is not necessarily an indication of its collectability.*

redundant ADJ If you are made **redundant**, your employer tells you to leave because your job is no longer necessary or because your employer cannot afford to keep paying you. • *My husband was made redundant late last year.*

plagiarism N-UNCOUNT **Plagiarism** is the practice of using or copying someone else's idea or work and pretending that you thought of it or created it. • *Now he's in real trouble. He's accused of plagiarism.*

awkwardly ADV When someone moves **awkwardly**, they move in an unnatural, clumsy way. • *He fell awkwardly and went down in agony clutching his right knee.*

Unit 12

grocery (groceries) N-COUNT **Groceries** are foods you buy at a supermarket such as flour, sugar, and tinned foods.

consumer (consumers) N-COUNT A **consumer** is a person who buys things or uses services. • *...improving public services and consumer rights.*

impulse ADJ An **impulse** buy or **impulse** purchase is something that you decide to buy when you see it, although you had not planned to buy it. • *The curtains were an impulse buy.*

resist (resists, resisting, resisted) VERB If you **resist** doing something, or **resist** the temptation to do it, you stop yourself from doing it although you would like to do it. • *She cannot resist giving him advice.*

tactic (tactics) N-COUNT **Tactics** are the methods that you choose to use in order to achieve what you want in a particular situation. • *What sort of tactics will the President use to rally the people behind him?*

circulation (circulations) N-COUNT The **circulation** of a newspaper or magazine is the number of copies that are sold each time it is produced. • *The Daily News once had the* highest circulation of any daily in the country.

perception (perceptions) N-COUNT Your **perception of** something is the way that you think about it or the impression you have of it. • *He is interested in how our perceptions of death affect the way we live.*

Unit 13

committee (committees) N-COUNT [with sing or pl verb] A **committee** is a group of people who meet to make decisions or plans for a larger group or organization that they represent. • *My reasons were stated in writing and circulated to all committee members.*

warden (wardens) N-COUNT A **warden** is a person who is responsible for a particular place or thing, and for making sure that the laws or regulations that relate to it are obeyed. • *Game wardens were appointed to enforce hunting laws in New Hampshire.*

welfare N-UNCOUNT The **welfare** of a person or group is their health, comfort, and happiness. • *He was the head of a charity for the welfare of children.*

resident (residents) N-COUNT The **residents** of a house or area are the people who live there. • *The Archbishop called upon the government to build more low cost homes for local residents.*

ball (balls) N-COUNT A **ball** is a large formal social event at which people dance. • *The college celebrated its birthday with a huge and very well organised May Ball in aid of Charities for Children.*

catering N-UNCOUNT **Catering** is the activity of providing food and drink for a large number of people, for example at weddings and parties. • *He recently did the catering for a presidential reception.*

quote (quotes) N-COUNT A **quote for** a piece of work is the price that someone says they will charge you to do the work. • *Always get a written quote for any repairs needed.*

Unit 14

verbal ADJ You use **verbal** to indicate that something is expressed in speech rather than in writing or action. • *We have a verbal agreement with her.*

resolve (resolves, resolving, resolved) VERB To **resolve** a problem, argument, or difficulty means to find a solution to it. [FORMAL] • *We must find a way to resolve these problems before it's too late.*

attentive ADJ Someone who is **attentive** is helpful and polite. • *The staff is well trained in courteous and attentive service to each and every guest.*

atmosphere N-SING The **atmosphere** of a place is the general impression that you get of it. • *Pale wooden floors and plenty of natural light add to the relaxed atmosphere.*

assurance (assurances) N-VAR If you give someone an **assurance that** something is true or will happen, you say that it is definitely true or will definitely happen, in order to make them feel less worried. • *He would like an assurance that other forces will not move into the territory.*

service N-UNCOUNT The level or standard of **service** provided by an organization or company is the amount or quality of the work it can do for you. • *We are trying to maintain these high levels of service.*

exaggerate (exaggerates, exaggerating, exaggerated) VERB If you **exaggerate**, you indicate that something is, for example, worse or more important than it really is. • *Sheila admitted that she did sometimes exaggerate the demands of her job.*

Unit 15

challenging ADJ A **challenging** task or job requires great effort and determination. • *Mike found a challenging job as a computer programmer.*

versatile ADJ If you say that a person is **versatile**, you approve of them because they have many different skills. [APPROVAL] • *He had been one of the game's most versatile athletes.*

demanding ADJ A **demanding** job or task requires a lot of your time, energy, or attention. • *He found he could no longer cope with his demanding job.*

till (tills) N-COUNT In a shop or other place of business, a **till** is a counter or cash register where money is kept, and where customers pay for what they have bought. [BRIT] • *...long queues at tills that make customers angry.*

able (abler, ablest) ADJ Someone who is **able** is very clever or very good at doing something. • *...one of the brightest and ablest members of the government.*

competent ADJ Someone who is **competent** is efficient and effective. • *He was a loyal, distinguished and very competent civil servant.*

synchronized swimming N-UNCOUNT **Synchronized swimming** is a sport in which two or more people perform complicated and carefully planned movements in water in time to music.

Unit 16

hire (hires, hiring, hired) VERB If you **hire** someone, you employ them or pay them to do a particular job for you. • *The rest of the staff have been hired on short-term contracts.*

cocktail (cocktails) N-COUNT A **cocktail** is an alcoholic drink which contains several ingredients. • *On arrival, guests are offered wine or a champagne cocktail.*

complement (complements, complementing, complemented) VERB If one thing **complements** another, it goes well with the other thing and makes its good qualities more noticeable. • *Nutmeg, parsley and cider all complement the flavour of these beans well.*

innovation N-UNCOUNT **Innovation** is the introduction of new ideas, methods, or things. • *We must promote originality and encourage innovation.*

single-handed ADV If you do something **single-handed**, you do it on your own, without help from anyone else. • *I brought up my seven children single-handed.*

drive N-UNCOUNT If you say that someone has **drive**, you mean they have energy and determination. • *John will be best remembered for his drive and enthusiasm.*

productivity N-UNCOUNT **Productivity** is the rate at which goods are produced. • *The third-quarter results reflect continued improvements in productivity.* • *His method of obtaining a high level of productivity is demanding.*

Unit 17

wind (winds, winding, wound) VERB If a road, river, or line of people **winds** in a particular direction, it goes in that direction with a lot of bends or twists in it. • *The Moselle winds through some 160 miles of tranquil countryside.*

graze (grazes, grazing, grazed) VERB When animals **graze**, they eat the grass or other plants that are growing in a particular place. • *...a large herd of grazing animals.*

spectacular ADJ Something that is **spectacular** is very impressive or dramatic. • ...*spectacular views of the Sugar Loaf Mountain.*

lodge (lodges) N-COUNT A **lodge** is a house or hut in the country or in the mountains where people stay on holiday, especially when they want to shoot or fish. • ...*a ski lodge.*

hitch (hitches, hitching, hitched) VERB If you **hitch**, **hitch** a lift, or **hitch** a ride, you hitchhike. [INFORMAL] • *There was no garage in sight, so I hitched a lift into town.*

flustered ADJ If you are **flustered**, you feel nervous and confused and cannot concentrate on what you are doing. • *She was so flustered that she forgot her reply.*

snake (snakes, snaking, snaked) VERB Something that **snakes** in a particular direction goes in that direction in a line with a lot of bends. [LITERARY] • *The road snaked through forested mountains.*

Unit 18

developer (developers) N-COUNT A **developer** is someone who develops something such as an idea, a design, or a product. • ...*a software developer.*

upgrade (upgrades, upgrading, upgraded) VERB If equipment or services **are upgraded**, they are improved or made more efficient. • *Medical facilities are being reorganized and upgraded.*

marathon (marathons) N-COUNT A **marathon** is a race in which people run a distance of 26 miles, which is about 42 km. • ...*running in his first marathon.*

terminology (terminologies) N-VAR The **terminology** of a subject is the set of special words and expressions used in connection with it. • ...*gastritis, which in medical*

terminology means an inflammation of the stomach.

succinct ADV If something is expressed **succinctly**, it is said or written clearly and in few words. • *He succinctly summed up his manifesto as 'Work hard, train hard and play hard'.*

hyperlink (hyperlinks) N-COUNT In an HTML document, a **hyperlink** is a link to another part of the document or to another document. Hyperlinks are shown as words with a line under them. [COMPUTING]

dominate (dominates, dominating, dominated) VERB To **dominate** a situation means to be the most powerful or important person or thing in it. • *The book is expected to dominate the best-seller lists.*

Unit 19

initially ADV **Initially** means soon after the beginning of a process or situation, rather than in the middle or at the end of it. • *Forecasters say the weather may not be as bad as they initially predicted.*

ideally ADV If you say that someone or something is **ideally** suited, **ideally** located, or **ideally** qualified, you mean that they are as well suited, located, or qualified as they could possibly be. • *The hotel is ideally situated for country walks.*

cleanliness N-UNCOUNT **Cleanliness** is the degree to which people keep themselves and their surroundings clean. • *Many of Britain's beaches fail to meet minimum standards of cleanliness.*

exemplary ADJ If you describe someone or something as **exemplary**, you think they are extremely good. • *His behaviour has been exemplary.*

fit N-SING If something is a good **fit**, it fits well. • *Eventually he was happy that the sills and doors were a reasonably good fit.*

ghastly ADJ If you describe someone or something as **ghastly**, you mean that you find them very unpleasant. [INFORMAL] • *It was the worst week of my life. It was ghastly.*

wilt (wilts, wilting, wilted) VERB If a plant **wilts**, it gradually bends downwards and becomes weak because it needs more water or is dying. • *The roses wilted the day after she bought them.*

Unit 20

stylish ADJ Someone or something that is **stylish** is smart, elegant, and fashionable. • ...*a varied choice of stylish designs.*

fabric (fabrics) N-VAR **Fabric** is cloth or other material produced by weaving together cotton, nylon, wool, silk, or other threads. Fabrics are used for making things such as clothes, curtains, and sheets. • ...*small squares of red cotton fabric.*

stitching N-UNCOUNT **Stitching** is a row of stitches that have been sewn in a piece of cloth. • *A star was done in red stitching.*

equally ADV **Equally** means to the same degree or extent. • *All these techniques are equally effective.*

spacious ADJ A **spacious** room or other place is large in size or area, so that you can move around freely in it. • *The house has a spacious kitchen and dining area.*

preference N-UNCOUNT If you **give preference to** someone with a particular qualification or feature, you choose them rather than someone else. • *The Pentagon will give preference to companies which do business electronically.*

rating (ratings) N-COUNT A **rating** of something is a score or measurement of how good or popular it is. • ...*a value-for-money rating of ten out of ten.*

Unit 1   Emails to friends

Understanding

Nicole asks Katy (**1**) to tell her all about how it feels to be a homeowner, and (**2**) what she thinks about Nicole moving in with some friends from work.

Writing appropriately

1

1	How's it going?	How are you?
2	so typical...	This happens all the time. *OR* I expected this to happen.
3	You won't believe this, but...	I have some news that will surprise you.
4	Write soon.	Please write to me soon.
5	Miss you	I miss you *OR* I wish you were here with me.

2

1 Hi! *OR* Yo! *OR* Hey!
2 What's up? *OR* How's it going? *OR* How are things? *OR* How're you doing?
3 I don't get it. *OR* What's that all about??????
4 What's the story? *OR* Tell me all about it. *OR* What's going on?
5 Miss you. *OR* Wish you were here. *OR* Can't wait to see you!

3 1 a   2 d   3 c   4 b

Language focus

1 should   2 will   3 can   4 might   5 can *OR* could

Get writing

1 Sample answers:

1 Hi Colin. I'm Rachel – remember me? We met at your friend Estelle's art show recently. Anyway, you very kindly mentioned that you were having a party this weekend, and I wondered if it would be ok for me to come along?
All the best, Rachel
2 Hey Miguel. All the stuff that's happening in your job sounds awful – poor you! Is there anything I can do to help out?
All my love, Nancy
3 Simone, You are not going to believe this, but – you remember that girl that Mark likes (the really pretty

one)? Well this morning when he was walking the dog in the park, he saw her sitting under a tree, and – this is hilarious – the dog ran straight up to her and began wagging its tail and barking! What do you think of that – could it be love?
Give me a call later, Maggie.

4 Hi Dom. Um, I'm really sorry to have to tell you this, but I'm afraid I managed to rip that T-shirt of yours that I borrowed. Really sorry about that, mate. Tell me where you got it and I'll buy you a new one. I'll sort it.
Anyway, see you soon. Sorry again! Kevin

5 Hi Martin. Long time no see! It's been far too long if you ask me. Time I came round to yours for a coffee and a catch up, maybe? By the way, I hear you've moved in with Sara. How is she doing these days?
All the best, Yishay

2 Sample answer:

From: katy.alvarez@cmail.com
Sent: 02 April 2012
To: nic.moreau99@dotmail.com
Subject: Re: New job!

Nicole!

Congratulations on the new job! It was great to hear from you and I'm so glad things are going well.

To answer your question – being a homeowner at last feels amazing! The apartment is beginning to feel like a proper home. We unpacked the very last box yesterday afternoon, then went to that amazing Thai restaurant on Bayard Street to celebrate. Do you remember it? The food was fantastic; I ate far too much, as usual! I wish you could have been there with us – it just wasn't the same without you.

Looking for a flat of your own sounds great, but I think you should take things slowly and get to know your friends a little better first. You've got plenty of time and anything can happen!

Keep in touch,

Love, Katy

Unit 2   Texting

Understanding

Problem: Anita's train is delayed, so she will be late for the film.

Solution: They will go to the restaurant early instead of going to the film. Dominik changes the restaurant reservation.

Looking more closely

1   Answers will vary.
2   Answers will vary, but texts are generally shorter, more personal, less grammatically correct, less formal and contain more shortened words.
3   Answers will vary, but texts often contain shortened words and emoticons to convey ideas quickly and easily.

Language focus

1

Train delayed 30mins. = My train has been delayed by 30 minutes.

We'll miss first part of film, won't we? = We'll miss the first part of the film, won't we?

Sorry. = I'm sorry.

We could skip film and go straight to restaurant? = We could skip (miss) the film and go straight to the restaurant, couldn't we? *OR* Could we skip the film and go straight to the restaurant?

Perfect. = That's perfect.

What time table booked for – can you change? = What time have you booked the table for? Can you change the time?

9pm. = I have booked the table for 9pm.

Changed booking. = I have changed the booking.

See u outside restaurant at 7. = I will see you outside the restaurant at 7 o'clock.

2

1   ~~My~~ car ~~has~~ broken down. ~~I~~ will be late for dinner.
2   What time is ~~the~~ meeting?
3   Can you buy ~~some~~ milk? ~~I~~ think we've run out.

4   ~~I~~ will be late for work. ~~I'm~~ sorry.
5   ~~The~~ restaurant ~~is~~ fully booked. What should we do?

Language Notes:

Not all prepositions in a sentence are function words. In Sentences 1 and 4 'for' adds meaning and leaving it out would be confusing.

Some sentences contain only content words. For example: 'What should we do?' Leaving out any of these words could confuse the reader.

3   1 you   2 be   3 laughing out loud *OR* lots of love

4   1 u   2 tho   3 BTW   4 u   5 OMG!   6 gr8   7 C u
8   cd.   9 LOL

5   Sample answers:

1   C u tomorrow.
2   How r u?
3   Saw John yesterday. He told me a gr8. story. LOL!

Get writing

1   Sample answers:

1   Just heard your job news. Congratulations! Fantastic news! Well done! Spk soon, R.
2   Can't find house keys. Do u have spares? Pls call asap. Bx
3   Will be a little late for work. Slept in – sorry! Frank.
4   Beatta Grace was born today at 03.18, 7lbs 6oz. Mum and baby both doing great. Dad is exhausted! Nico
5   Can't make Tues. What about next Thurs? You can let me know. R.
6   Can we talk? Sx

2   Sample answers:

1   Oh no! Will B with u soon. Jump up and down 2 stay warm!
2   Hello. Busy now. Can I call u in 1 hr? Thx!
3   How late r u gonna b? We r hungry!

Unit 3   Instant Messaging

Language focus

1

4 = for, probs = problems, ☺ = I'm enjoying this/this is fun, LOL = laughing out loud, M = Marika, mins = minutes, v. = very, sec. = second, sbd. = somebody, abt. = about

2

1   Sorry to stop you …, Hold on a sec.
2   Just to change the subject …

3   Back! Sorry, you were asking about …

3   1 R   2 CS   3 CS   4 R   5 I   6 I

Writing appropriately

1   Sample answers:

1   Start by apologizing to the people around you, for example: 'Could you just excuse me for one moment? I really need to reply to this very quickly.'

Type to your friend, for example: 'Sorry. In a meeting now. Will call u ASAP.'

2 Just a sec. / Back shortly. (Don't waste time writing long explanations if there is an emergency to deal with. You also don't want to scare the person you are talking to!)

3 Hey Cassie. Sorry to interrupt, but I'm starving. Can we chat after lunch?

2

1 laughing OR big grin
2 heart OR love
3 excitement OR jumping for joy
4 surprise OR shocked face
5 broken heart OR no love

Unit 4   Invitations and RSVPs

Understanding

This is an invitation to a wedding (Fayah and Neil are getting married).

Looking more closely

1 Wells Manor House.   2 Frensham Hall.
3 1 May 2012.   4 7 July 2012.

Writing appropriately

1 1 a   2 d   3 f   4 e   5 c   6 b

2 1 pleasure   2 invited   3 delighted
4 present   5 honour

3 1 join   2 surprise   3 21st   4 celebrating   5 late
6 17   7 forward   8 RSVP

4 1 Formal   2 Informal   3 Formal   4 Informal

Get writing

1 Sample answer:

From: roxana.gordan@dotmail.com
Sent: 10 April 2012
To: rico99@flymail.com
Subject: Juliana's 21st

Hi Rico,

I'll be there. I can't wait! Do you need any help?

Roxi x

Get writing

1 Sample answers:

1 No probs. I'll change booking.
2 In bar next 2 restaurant. C u there!

2 Sample answers:

1 Give me a minute too – just finishing off essay.
2 Back! What's happening?
3 No probs, will do. Now that's dealt with, what time does the baseball start tomorrow?
4 You: Sorry u 2, gotta go. Pizza delivery!

2 Sample answer:

> Dear Fayah and Neil,
>
> We will be delighted to attend your wedding ceremony on Saturday 7 July at 2pm. Unfortunately, we are sad to say that we will not be able to join you for the celebrations afterwards at Frensham Hall Hotel. I'm afraid we have made some travel arrangements that we can't rearrange.
>
> However, we are thrilled to receive an invitation to your big day and are really looking forward to joining you for (perhaps) the most important part of it!
>
> With warmest wishes,
>
> Jane and Kev Morgan

9 Sample answer:

> Professor Alison Hylands
> is retiring from Brockwell University's Chemistry Department after 25 years' service.
>
> You are invited to attend Professor Hylands's retirement party on Thursday 9 August 2012, from 7pm until late at Rizzo's Italian Restaurant, 31 Byres Lane, Brockwell
>
> RSVP by
> Thursday 2 August 2012
> (with any dietary requirements) to:
> Brian Barker
> Brockwell University Chemistry Department

Unit 5   Thank-you letters

Understanding

Katerina made a special quilt (a type of blanket) for Mira, with the characters from one of her favourite books sewn into it.

Lynne, Alec and Mira are very impressed by how beautiful the quilt is, and very grateful to Katerina for making it.

Looking more closely

- all the way from Germany! (surprise)

She is absolutely delighted. (pleasure)

What a good memory you have! (surprise)

Katerina, you are so talented! (admiration)

… you have put such a huge amount of time and care into making this quilt perfect. (admiration, gratitude)

Yours is the kindest and most thoughtful gift Mira has ever received, and I know she will treasure it for many years to come. (gratitude/pleasure)

With love and thanks to both of you. (gratitude)

Writing appropriately

Sample answers:

2   Thank you so much for organizing such a wonderful party!
3   You cooked the nicest dinner I've had in ages!
4   You worked so hard organizing the party. It was the best party I've ever had!
5   The gift was absolutely beautiful and I like it very, very much!

Language Focus

1

Dear Josie,

I wanted to write and thank you so much for the fabulous party you organized for my 40th [simple past]. I had no idea you had anything planned [simple past + past perfect]– it was such a surprise [simple past]! Everything was perfect [simple past] – it was great to see all the girls together again [past simple]. The food was amazing [past simple], and that champagne was spectacular [past simple]! Most importantly, the birthday cake you made for me was [past simple] the best I have ever tasted [present perfect]. (And I've tasted quite a few in my 40 years!) [present perfect] I've been telling everyone here what a fantastic night it was [present perfect continuous] and showing them the photos [present perfect continuous]. It just couldn't have been better [present perfect] – I felt so special [past simple]. Thank you for all your hard work, secret planning, and for all the thought and care you put into the evening [past simple]. It was the happiest night of my life [past simple]. I'll remember it forever!

With lots of love and thanks to my beautiful best friend,

Andrea Xxx

2   Sample answers:

1   Thank you for the gift of the tickets – I'd wanted to see *Carmen* for a long time!

2   Thanks for organizing the lovely party – I hadn't expected anyone to remember my birthday!
3   I'd always wanted to go to Russia, so I was amazed when you told me we were going!
4   I had thought my car couldn't possibly be fixed, so I am very grateful to you for proving me wrong!

Writing more appropriately

Sample answers:

1   (OTT) Your gift of a new electric kettle was very thoughtful. It was the most useful gift we received at our wedding, and we have already put it in our new kitchen.
2   (LW) Thank you so much for organizing my very enjoyable leaving party. I had the best time I've had in years!
3   (OTT) It was very kind of you to buy me lunch last week. I had a really nice time – thank you!
4   (LW) Thank you so much for looking after our house while we were on holiday. Two weeks is a long time and we are very grateful for all your hard work. Thanks especially for tidying the house – it looked lovely when we got back.

Get writing

1   Sample answers:

1   Thank you very, very much for the wonderful painting you bought me. I had wanted a painting by this artist for years – how did you know?!
2   I enjoyed the party so much! Thanks again for all your hard work, and for managing to keep it a secret for such a long time!
3   I had thought I'd probably never drive that car again, so thank you very much for fixing it. I really appreciate all your hard work.
4   The crystal vase is absolutely exquisite. It must be the most beautiful gift I've ever received!

2

> Dear Uncle Pete,
>
> I wanted to write and thank you for fixing the brake pads on my car last weekend. I wouldn't have known where to start to fix them myself, and the garage estimate was really expensive. You saved me so much cash – thank you!
>
> Your time and effort didn't just save me money, by the way – because I got the car fixed so quickly, I was able to drive to Birmingham to hand-deliver my application for a new job (just before the closing date), and I've got an interview!
>
> Thanks again for all your hard work and expertise – you're the best.
>
> Rob.

Unit 6   Postcards

Understanding

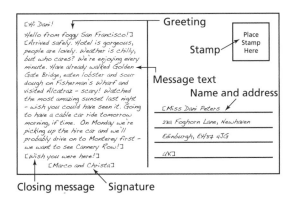

Greeting

Stamp

Message text

Name and address

Closing message   Signature

Writing clearly

1

1   The hotel is gorgeous and the people are lovely.
2   The weather is chilly, but who cares?
3   We have already walked the Golden Gate Bridge ... and visited Alcatraz – which was scary *OR* which we found scary!
4   We are going to have a cable car ride tomorrow morning, if there is time *OR* if we have time.

2   Sample answers:

1   Weather here's been terrible! *OR* Weather terrible.
2   Been having a brilliant holiday.
3   So far have visited Cairo and Pyramids.
4   Wish you could've seen giant squid at the aquarium – terrifying!

3

1 C   2 C   3 G   4 G   5 G   6 C   7 G

Looking more closely

1 ✗   2 ✓   3 ✗   4 ✗   5 ✓   6 ✓   7 ✓   8 ✗

Language focus

Sample answers:

1   We've been learning to SCUBA dive – it's challenging!
2   Had terrible jetlag for first 3 days – feeling better now.
3   Visited the Eiffel Tower – beautiful!
4   Going to visit the art gallery tomorrow – exciting!

Get writing

1, 2

Answers will vary.

3   Sample answer:

Hi Kate and Marcus!

Having a fabulous time in Oz! Flight long, but great seats. Staying in beautiful hotel with view of Sydney Opera House. Weather perfect for sightseeing – bright, warm, not too hot. The Aussies are so friendly – brilliant accent too. Had surfing lessons yesterday then beach barbeque – amazing. Trying a new seafood restaurant tonight before checking out nightlife. Will need relaxing day by the pool tomorrow!

Wish you were here, guys!

Eleni and Zander xx

Unit 7   Writing notes

Understanding

1

The notes are broken down into groups/headings.
The writer has used stars (*) to show the most important notes.
Notes are short and easy to understand.

2

1   Feed the cat half a tin of cat food twice a day; keep the water bowl clean and full.
2   Don't let the cat out of the house.
3   Every day after the cat's last feed.
4   In the cupboard to the left of the dishwasher.

5   Buy some more – your friend will give you the money when they return.

3

Services: cleaner, towels replaced daily, laundry service

Responsibilities: lock the gate each night and if you leave during the day, no smoking in the villa

Looking more closely

1   Saturday and Sunday
2   Speak to the cleaner
3   In the garden and on the balcony areas
4   Playa Repic

Language focus

1 with   2 without   3 somebody   4 something
5 chapter   6 page/pages   7 number/numbers
8 about   9 versus (meaning 'against')
10 because   11 minimum   12 maximum

Get writing

1   Answers depend on students.

2   Sample answer:

Thanks for looking after the house.

- *Please water the plants in living room, bedroom, and kitchen, every three days if possible. Don't water the plants in bathroom or they will die!*
- *Keep heating on if it's okay with you. If we turn it off we always have trouble getting it to restart. We will fix that when we get back.*
- *To use shower: Firstly turn on the water (button at bottom) then turn dial at the top towards the right to increase temperature. If you do it the other way round you might get scalded.*
- *We have left some fresh coffee beans for you – you must try our new grinder and coffee*

---

machine – they are awesome. There is also an amazing deli just round the corner that bakes fresh croissants every morning. Take first left as you leave the house, then turn right onto Savoy place. It's the third shop on your right. Enjoy croissants with coffee.

- *Lastly, if you are unable to stay for any reason, please let our neighbour, Mrs May, at No 54 know. She has a key and has looked after the house before. If you can't let her know in person, her number is 01903 246 876. I think that's it. Any problems, text me on 07743 342 856.*

3   Sample answer:

1   Richard Hart, Head of Linguistics Dept Keele Uni. Call on 01463 435 291, 9–5 asap re. application. Applic. w/o research proposal – pp missing? NB Must call in < a week b/c applic cd be rejected.
2   Flat 63 Orchard Brae, Bromley. 3 beds, £150 pcm < others. 5 mins walk max from Tube. Call Est Agent 01395 456 989. Have < week to view, decide & pay deposit. NB Ask abt parking.

Unit 8   Making polite enquiries

Language focus

1

1   The writer uses 'Ms', which is a polite way to address a woman when you aren't sure if she is 'Miss' or 'Mrs'. Note: some women always use 'Ms' instead of 'Miss' or 'Mrs'. If you know which title she prefers, it is polite to use that one.
2   He calls her website 'excellent'. Offering praise is a nice way to start a polite letter or email.
3   He uses the modal verb 'would' (e.g. 'I would like to make a booking…'). 'Would' is a polite way to make a request. Without it, requests can sound more like demands. Contrast 'I want to make a booking' with 'I would like to make a booking'. The second is politer because it suggests that the writer does not expect the reader to do as he asks. What he is really saying is 'I would like to make a booking… but I will understand if it isn't possible.'
4   He uses polite phrases such as 'I hope that this is acceptable', 'please' and 'would be greatly appreciated'. There are a number of common polite phrases. It is good to learn a selection of these to add to polite requests.
5   He uses an 'if' clause to show he understands that what he is asking for may not be possible. ('If you are happy for us to stay at the villa, please let me know.') In this example, he is using the first conditional, but we can also use the second

conditional (e.g. 'If we arrived on Wednesday instead of Thursday, would that be easier for you?').
6   He finishes the email with two very common polite statements: 'I look forward to your reply' is a standard line at the end of emails with a business element. 'Kind regards' is a polite and friendly way to finish an email to someone whose name you know. 'Yours faithfully' is a polite way to finish an email to someone whose name you don't know.

2   Sample answers:

1   I wonder if you could call me?
2   Please could you call me?
3   I wonder if you would mind giving me your address?
4   Could you possibly help me to find a cleaner?
5   Would you mind telling me where the garage is?

3   Sample answers:

1 I'd like   2 would   3 would/could, I'd
4 are   5 I'd, would/could

Language note: to avoid using 'if' twice in the same sentence, the writer has used 'whether' instead.

4

1   The email in Exercise 4 is more informal.
2   The email in Exercise 4 uses more contracted words (e.g 'I've').
3   The email in Exercise 1 uses full names and titles.

5

I would like to …
I hope that this is acceptable …
I would like to enquire whether/if …
Would it be possible to …
If you are happy …, please …
… would be greatly appreciated.
Kind regards
I was wondering whether/if it would be possible to …
If it's not too much trouble …
Does that all sound okay with you?
Looking forward to …

Get writing

1 Sample answers:

1 Could you possibly tell me where I might be able to park my car near the college?
2 If you could let me take next Monday off, that would be greatly appreciated.
3 I wonder if you could let me know whether there is a waiting list for tickets?
4 Please could I exchange an item of clothing that is too small for me?

2 Sample answer:

> Dear Ms Harcourt,
>
> I am interested in your evening study course 'Basic Computing Level 1' and wonder whether I could ask for a few further details before I apply.
>
> Firstly, may I ask if there are still places available for the course? If so, could you tell me when it is held and how often it meets? I am afraid that I am unfamiliar with the campus, so if you also could let me know where the course is held and perhaps include some directions, I would be extremely grateful.

> Lastly, would it be possible to let me know the total cost for the course, and your preferred method of payment? I can pay in advance if that would help secure my place.
>
> Please do not hesitate to get in touch if you need any further information from me in order to register my application.
>
> With thanks for your help and advice,
>
> Florin Ivan.

3 Sample answer:

> Hi Alec!
>
> How are you doing? I hope you are really well. We are fine – too busy as always but we've got a holiday planned soon, so that will be great.
>
> I hope you don't mind me writing to ask, but I was wondering whether you remember those wine glasses I lent you for your housewarming party last year. (That was such a great night by the way!) There were twelve glasses in total, with tall stems and cut glass. Well, the reason I mention them is that we are having an anniversary party next month and would really like to use them. If it's okay with you, I could pop round for them next week when you're free.
>
> I hope you don't mind – the glasses were a 21st birthday gift from my mum so I'd better keep an eye on them!
>
> It would be great if you could let me know when would be a good time to pop round. I'll look forward to seeing you next week sometime!
>
> Love,
>
> Christina
>
> x

Unit 9   Giving instructions

Understanding

Ashmi and Nikhil are probably driving to the party in a car. The instructions are quite detailed, and they mention fairly long distances like 'follow this road for about half a mile'. The instructions contain information that applies specifically to driving, e.g. 'at the roundabout, take the first exit…'. The final instruction tells them to 'turn into the driveway slowly', which you would do with a car, and mentions the parking space.

Looking more closely

1 1 h 2 g 3 a 4 b 5 c 6 d 7 f 8 e

2 1 car 2 train 3 on foot 4 on foot 5 bus 6 car 7 train 8 bus

Language focus

More than one answer is correct. The first and second steps can be done in either order, as can the third and fourth steps.

First / Firstly, clear the area where you want to put up the tent. Get rid of rocks, sticks, or other sharp objects.

Second / Secondly, unpack and separate the tent from the tent poles and tent pegs.

After that / Next / Then, you should put down the tent in the area that you have already cleared and unfold it there. Make sure that the top is facing up. Pull on the edges to fit the tent into the spot you have cleared.

After that / Next / Then, assemble the tent poles.

After that / Next / Then, insert the tent poles into the sleeves around the edges of the tent. Keep going until all the main poles are connected to the tent.

Finally / Lastly, to secure your tent, use the tent pegs to secure the ropes around the tent. This will stop your tent blowing away in the wind!

Writing clearly

Sample answer:
First, lay the sheet flat on the mattress, with the longest sides of the sheet next to the longest sides of the mattress. Next, pull one corner of the sheet around the closest corner of the mattress. Then move around the bed to the diagonally opposite corner and pull the sheet over it. Finally, repeat with the other two corners.

Get Writing

1 Sample answers:

1 By bus
Go to stand number 3 outside Brixton Station and catch the Number 27 to Norwood Bus Garage. After about 10 minutes, get off at the stop outside Norwood Fire Station. My house is just around the corner on Catford Road. The whole journey should take about 15 minutes.
2 By car
Go up Brixton Road and turn down Shakespeare Road (avoid Electric Avenue because of the roadworks). When you get to Herne Hill, drive south along the edge of Brockwell Park. When you get to Tulse Hill Roundabout, bear right and then take the second exit. Catford Road is the first turn on the left. It should only take you ten minutes to get here.
3 On foot
Walk up Shakespeare Road and then head through the centre of Brockwell Park (make sure you set off before 6 because they close the park when it gets dark). When you get to the other side of the park, come out of the gate near Deronda Road, then cross over and head down Argyll Avenue. Keep walking for about ten minutes until you get to the junction with Catford Road. The whole journey usually takes me about thirty minutes.

2 Sample answers:

How to use the coffee machine

First, check it is plugged in at the wall socket and switched on.

Second, put a filter paper into the cone at the top of the machine (filter papers are in a box next to the coffee machine).

After that, put three scoops of coffee into the filter paper (coffee is in the fridge).

Then, press the 'on' switch at the front of the machine.

Next, fill the jug with cold water from the tap and pour it into the slot at the back of the machine.

Finally, wait five minutes and you will have a lovely cup of coffee!

How to turn on the heating

First, you'll need to turn on the boiler. It's in the kitchen cupboard next to the sink. Turn the dial to the left until the red light goes on. Next, find the control box in the hall. It's a little white box on the wall next to the stairs. Open the cover and press the < and > buttons until you get the temperature you want. Please don't forget to turn the boiler off when you leave!

How to lock and unlock the front door

1 Use the big gold key in the mortice lock at the bottom of the door. Turn it clockwise to lock and anti-clockwise to unlock. It's a bit stiff but it works fine if you pull the door handle towards you as you turn it.
2 Use the silver key in the lock above the door handle. Turn it anti-clockwise to lock and clockwise to unlock.

What to do in an emergency

1 Call me first, on my mobile and/or landline.
2 If I don't answer and it's really urgent (e.g. burst water pipe), call Janis, my landlady. She lives close by and her number is 020 317 88795.

3 Sample answer:

> Hi girls!
>
> So, here are the details for Maria's surprise 30th birthday party …
>
> *WHERE TO MEET*
>
> Our venue will be 'The Apartment' (57 Whitelinks Plaza, Brighton BN41 2AJ). We will meet there on Saturday 3 September at 2pm.
>
> *WHAT TO DO*
>
> I need you to do four things to help the day go smoothly.
>
> 1 Firstly, buy a small gift for Maria that reminds you of her, and we'll embarrass her by telling her how great she is.
> 2 After that, sort out your outfit – wear either pink or black.
> 3 Next, make sure you bring your own bottle for dinner.
> 4 Finally – be on time! I'm bringing her to the venue at 2:05 exactly, so don't be late!!!
>
> Do not tell her anything about it. It's a surprise!
> Looking forward to seeing you there!
>
> Andra x

Unit 10   Writing to confirm arrangements

Understanding

Hugo is confirming: the date and length of the stay at the holiday villa, the number of people in the group,

that Ms Valente is happy for children to stay at the villa, the time of their arrival, when and where to collect the keys, that arrangements for disabled facilities, the amount of the deposit and the method of payment.

Writing clearly

1 Possible answers:

1 As discussed/agreed, *OR* Just to confirm, *OR* Could you confirm that … *OR* Could I just check/confirm that …
2 Is that correct?
3 Could you confirm that … *OR* Could I just check/confirm that …
4 Just to confirm, *OR* Could you confirm that … *OR* Could I just check/confirm that …

2 Sample answers:

1 Could I just check that there are rooms available at your hotel this weekend?
2 I have been told that a payment will be made to my bank account this week. Is this correct?
3 As agreed, my order will be ready for collection tomorrow?

Language focus

Hugo justifies his choice by explaining that the taxi drive there is shorter and cheaper, and that the owner is extremely helpful.

Get writing

1 Sample answers:

1 Can I confirm that you are happy to deliver the sofa to me?
2 Just to confirm: you will be cleaning the house every Wednesday from 9am?

2 Sample answers:

1 I decided to buy the red sofa, because it was more comfortable than the black one. Not only that, but the black one was too small.
2 I've decided that we should buy the special ticket, rather than two separate tickets. That way, we can see the museum and the castle. Not only that, but it's cheaper and quicker.

3 Sample answer:

From: shazia@msc-designs.com
Sent: 14 March 2012
To: bookings@olivetree.com
Subject: Birthday Party Booking 27 March 2012

Hello again,

I am writing to finally confirm arrangements for our birthday party booking on 27 March 2012.

There will be ten adults in our party. Two have special dietary requirements – one is a vegetarian and one is allergic to nuts. Thank you for confirming by phone that you are able to cater for them appropriately.

As previously discussed, our party will arrive at 8.45 in order to eat promptly at 9pm. We need to pay the bill no later than 10.30pm as some of our party have long journeys to get home from the restaurant. If you anticipate any problems with these timings please do let me know soon.

As I also mentioned in our phone call, we have a birthday cake for one member of our party, Bianca Ortega, who will be 25 years old. I will deliver the birthday cake to the restaurant as agreed at 3pm on the afternoon of the 27th March. Could you ensure that the cake is brought out in the evening, with candles lit, when we have finished our main course? Thanks!

If you have any questions or need any more information, please email me!

With many thanks for your help,

Shazia Hazra

4 Sample answer:

From: shazia@msc-designs.com
Sent: 20 March 2012
To: Party People
Subject: Bianca's Birthday Party 27 March!

Hi guys,

I've just finalized arrangements for Bianca's birthday. I've made a block booking for us to go and see 'Not a Penny More' at 6.30 at the Showcase Cinema on Elm Street. It finishes at 8.20, which gives us more than enough time to walk to the restaurant for 8.45. That new action movie 'Storm Breaker' is on as well but it doesn't finish until 8.40, which is too late if we are going to get to the restaurant on time.

In the end I booked Olive Tree, the Italian place on Tottenham Avenue. The food is meant to be great and it's very near the cinema. I know you all like Chinese and I thought about booking the Golden Panda, but it was just too far away – the taxis would have been really expensive. I thought it would be nice to eat somewhere close enough to the cinema that we could walk there. That way we can stretch our legs and have a chat on the way before we sit down again.

Greg, Miranda – no problems about veggie meal and nut-free menu. I've got that all sorted.

Hope that's all okay with everyone – email me if not!

Love,

Shazia x

Unit 11   Writing a summary

Understanding

The summary is one paragraph, whereas the business report has two paragraphs. The summary omits some of the details in the report (e.g. instead of repeating that total sales fell by 9%, it simply says there was a drop in sales). The summary takes information contained in several sentences and condenses it into one. The summary paraphrases the report (it changes most of the words and uses different sentence structure and clauses).

Writing clearly

1

Thesis statement: Research shows shoppers spend more at Christmas after a tough financial year, though the biggest spenders may be those least able to afford it.

2

Answers will depend on which magazines or newspapers students choose.

Writing appropriately

1

1   Although it had a tough year in 2011 …
2   … there was a drop in sales.
3   … some staff were made redundant.
4   … will grow profits and keep staff happy.

2   Sample answers:

1   The countryside around the volcano was severely damaged when it erupted, and many people were killed.
2   Analysts predicted that share prices would grow further later this year, after they rose in the first quarter.
3   The press were told by the film's director that he would no longer be making any films.

Get writing

1   Sample answer:

Jane came into the office early that morning, around 7.45am, to do some extra work. She didn't notice that the cleaner was still washing the floor in the hallway, as she always did before anyone arrived for work. Jane stopped to have a quick chat with Bill, the night security guard at the reception desk, to ask him how his holiday had been. She then checked her watch and realized it was nearly 8.00am, so she quickly gathered up her briefcase and papers and ran towards the lift. She slipped on the wet floor and fell awkwardly onto her side, dropping her briefcase and papers. When the security guard and cleaner came over to help

her, Jane was holding her left shoulder and couldn't move that arm. The security guard was finishing work at 8am anyway, so he drove Jane to hospital to be checked immediately. Fortunately, Jane had only a bruise on her upper arm and had not broken any bones.

2   Source text:

The Apostrophe

Consider the poor apostrophe, so eager and willing, yet so often misunderstood. What's worse, so often in the wrong place at the wrong time. The pop industry is perhaps the most visibly guilty of its maltreatment. The apostrophe was publicly ensnared in the band name Hear'Say before the group did the right thing and broke up, releasing the innocent punctuation mark. Hijacked by an Australian band in 2002 it briefly adorned the unsettling title Scandal'Us. However, even they couldn't stand the guilt of its wrongful imprisonment. The ill-fated singers shuffled off shame-faced, leaving the apostrophe at the mercy of the next pop wannabe. And so it goes on.

Abuse of the apostrophe is, however, a symptom of its very character. It is obedient, enthusiastic, and capable of carrying out many important tasks. A bit like a spaniel, you might say. However that's where the analogy ends, because we are usually quite nice to spaniels.

The apostrophe first appeared in the English Language in the 16th century simply to mark omitted letters. The word's Greek root means 'turn away' and from that, 'omission' or 'elision'. Always one for a new trend, Shakespeare scattered it liberally throughout his plays to carry out that duty. Later, printers began to use it to mark possessives; first singular 'the boy's hat' and then plural 'the boys' hats'. Then, as we heaped ever more responsibility onto the wide-eyed apostrophe, everything went to hell in a handcart until, now, we are guilty of putting it to work in places it just shouldn't be. Think of cafés boasting of 'Freshly ground coffee's'. Shocking brutality. End it now by reading on.

Sample answer:

Thesis statement:

The apostrophe is often used wrongly in written English, possibly because it is so versatile and has such a long and varied history.

Outline note:

1   The apostrophe is often used wrongly, perhaps most often by the pop industry.
2   Its misuse may be a symptom of its versatility.

3   It has a long history, during which it has taken on more and more jobs.

Summary:

The apostrophe seems to appear in the wrong place very often. It is misused by many people, particularly those in the pop industry where it is often used to create innovative new names for pop bands.

The apostrophe seems to be so misused because it is a victim of its own versatility – it is used to carry

out many jobs in English, which may have led to confusion.

The apostrophe was first used in English in the 16th century to indicate where a letter had been missed out, which related to the meaning of the word in Greek. Then, printers started using it to denote possessives, first for singular nouns, then for plurals too. Then, as its use became more widespread, we began to get confused and now often use it wrongly.

Unit 12   Writing an article or essay

Understanding

The article is structured into four paragraphs, each of which deals with a different method for saving money on your grocery bill. By dividing the article up into smaller sections it becomes easier to read. The author also uses linking words like 'moreover' to join ideas together.

Language focus

1

The best thing to do if you want to save money on your grocery bills is to think ahead. That way, you can plan your meals for the week and list all the ingredients you will need to make them. This prevents expensive, last-minute trips to the supermarket for one dinner ingredient. You are far more likely to buy unnecessary items when you are in a rush.

Many consumers make savings by shopping online. <u>Despite the fact that</u> there is usually a delivery charge for online grocery deliveries, many people find online shopping saves both time and money. Impulse buys are easier to resist and bargains are often easier to spot. <u>In addition</u>, simply because consumers can see their bill adding up as they shop, they are far more likely to stick to the budget they intended.

Many consumers are finding that rising fuel costs are adding to their shopping bills, <u>because</u> they are driving miles away to shop at a 'cheaper' supermarket. **<u>Another option is</u> to consider shopping locally.** It is worthwhile checking the prices in your high street and calculating how much you could save by walking home with your shopping! <u>Moreover</u>, you will be supporting your own community too.

None of these tactics will work, <u>however,</u> unless you actually monitor your total household spending. To tightly control your spending, consider moving to online banking, where you can check your bank accounts daily, move money, and avoid costly bank charges as well.

2

1 Although   2 In spite of   3 Furthermore
4 On the other hand

Looking more closely

See the Answer key text for Language focus, Exercise 1. Topic sentences are in **bold**. Note that in the third paragraph, the topic sentence is the second sentence, not the first.

Writing clearly

Sample answers:

Paragraph 1: Diet experts are always advising us to eat more fruit and vegetables, but should we pay attention?

Paragraph 2: Not only can fruit and vegetables be expensive, some fruits contain a lot of sugar.

Paragraph 3: Despite this, the health benefits of eating fruit and vegetables are clear.

Paragraph 4: Overall, it seems that the experts are probably right.

Writing appropriately

1

The four paragraphs each talk about a different idea related to the main topic on saving money. Paragraph one talks about planning your shopping in advance, paragraph two talks about shopping online, paragraph three talks about shopping locally and the final paragraph talks about monitoring your overall budget. These ideas are all linked, but they are different enough that they need one paragraph each.

2

<u>The number of printed newspapers sold in the UK has fallen dramatically in recent years.</u>   —— Topic sentences

This has mainly been due to the popularity of online news sources, which are generally free to access. In addition, many people now get their news from social media sources such as Twitter.   —— Supporting sentences

<u>In spite of the shift to online news, many people continue to purchase printed newspapers and magazines.</u>   —— Topic sentences

Supporting sentences Some have even increased their circulation, perhaps because of the perception that online news sources are unreliable.

3 Sample answers:

1 Scientists predict time travel will be possible for humans
Possible paragraph structure: 1 – Introduction, 2 – facts about recent scientific discoveries related to time travel, 3 – comments from other scientists on the findings, 4 – conclusion/further information.

2 New smartphones are not as great as everyone thinks
1 – Introduction, 2 – why people think new smartphones are great, 3 – technological reasons why new smartphones aren't great, 4 – why the services provided by new smartphones aren't that great, 5 – conclusion.

Get writing

Sample answer:

Plan:

1	Introduction	4	Important items
2	Removal	5	Personal luggage
3	Clearing out	6	Conclusion

Topic sentences:

1 There are a few things to consider that can make your house move go according to plan, no matter how far you are travelling.
2 Choose a good removal company.
3 Make your house move a good reason to get rid of unwanted belongings.
4 Watch your belongings being packed and give specific instructions for fragile or valuable items.
5 Take as much personal luggage as you can.
6 Enjoy your travels.

Completed article:

Moving house is difficult for everyone, but moving abroad seems much harder. However, there are a few things to consider that can make your house move go according to plan, no matter how far you are travelling.

Choose a good removal company. Though it can take time, it is probably best to compare two or three companies before you make a final decision. Ask friends for recommendations. Some companies can move your belongings anywhere, which is very reassuring. However, companies that use partners abroad are cheaper. You must decide what is most important to you – a cost saving, or the simplicity of dealing with only one company.

Make your house move a good reason to get rid of unwanted belongings. Because you are starting a new life in a new country, you have a perfect opportunity to start again. Get rid of memorabilia that you would rather forget, sell things and give outdated clothes or furniture to charity. You will make money, save shipping costs and feel good too.

Watch your belongings being packed and give specific instructions for fragile or valuable items, as this will help reassure you and will make unpacking easier at your final destination. However, ensure that portable electronic equipment like iPads come with you personally, because you will need them throughout your move. In addition, important documents like passports and birth certificates should stay with you at all times too.

Take as much personal luggage as you can. Fortunately, many airlines will offer extra baggage if you tell them that you are moving abroad. Check the allowance before you fly and ask for more. While you should pack as much as you can, you must avoid going over your allowance or you will face an expensive fee.

Lastly, enjoy your travels – this is the start of your new life!

Unit 13   Writing formal notes and notices

Understanding

The purpose of the notice is:

- To warn local residents that thefts have occurred from houses.
- To advise local residents of how to protect themselves from theft.
- To give information about the neighbourhood welfare committee.
- To invite residents to attend community meetings.
- To give residents contact details and links to more information.

Looking more closely

1 It isn't clear exactly who the author is. The notice refers to 'our' and 'we', so it may have been written by several people. There is a telephone number for Nissa Laarsen, who may be the author, or simply the contact person for the group.

2 The notice has a headline, an introductory paragraph, some bullet points giving advice, another paragraph about the group, and then a selection of contact information and a weblink.

3 It is common to see notices like this in community buildings like town halls and libraries, often on a dedicated noticeboard. Notices like this one, which are relevant to a local community, are sometimes displayed as posters on telegraph poles or in other prominent locations.

Language focus

1

Residents are reminded of some simple precautions to prevent crime.

Keep all valuable items away from windows where they can be easily seen.

Your neighbourhood welfare committee was established in 2010 …

… all residents are invited to attend

Meeting minutes can be downloaded …

2

1   Some houses in the neighbourhood have been broken into (by thieves).
2   This notice was written by Marcia White.
3   Extra rubbish bins have been placed around the park (by the Council).

Writing appropriately

a 4   b 3   c 5   d 1   e 2

OR

1 d   2 e   3 b   4 a   5 c

Get writing

1   Sample answer:

> #### Notice to Residents: Vandalism of Wheelie Bins – Public Meeting
>
> Many residents have had their wheelie bins vandalized or tipped over in the past month by vandals who have been drinking. We are currently speaking to the police in order to resolve this problem entirely with their help.
>
> We are having a public meeting about this problem one Wednesday 10 October in the Community Hall at 7.30pm. All are invited to attend, whether you have been affected by this problem or not. Please bring your ideas and voice them at the meeting. Alternatively you can email/phone the meeting organizer, Erwin Strenke: Erwin@communityhelp.org.uk or Tel: 01287 557 992.

2   Sample answer:

> **Flat Meeting 1 May 2012**
> **17 White Street, Ampleforth.**
> Present: Mike, Candice, Eleni, Ibrahim, Anil.
> **First agenda item: Sharing the housework.**
>
> Discussion points:
>
> * Candice and Anil have felt for some time that they have been doing most of the cleaning, and that the others have not been taking enough responsibility for cleaning shared rooms like the bathroom, living room and kitchen.
> * Mike, Eleni and Ibrahim apologized and were willing to work things out.
>
> Decision: Mike will put together a cleaning rota and put it up in the kitchen for everyone to follow.
>
> **Second agenda item: Smoking in the house.**
>
> Discussion point:
>
> * All flatmates have been considering a total ban on smoking in the flat, with the full support of the two smokers Eleni and Ibrahim.
>
> Decision: An official smoking ban for flatmates and friends will start from tomorrow morning!
>
> **Any other business:**
>
> All flatmates are agreed that we should have a meal out together to celebrate our cleaning rota and smoke-free house. Please write your restaurant suggestions on the noticeboard for Saturday 17 May, along with agenda items for our next meeting on the same date.

Unit 14   A letter or email of complaint

Understanding

1   T
2   T
3   F (The main paragraph summarizes the complaint in detail).
4   T (The first paragraph mentions the writer's previous positive experiences at the restaurant.)

Writing appropriately

1

My family and I have always enjoyed the excellent food, attentive service and great atmosphere that the restaurant offers.

However, on Friday 30th March I had a very unpleasant dining experience at Lexington's.

… were told by a very rude waitress to wait at the bar until our table was ready.

She continued to be rude and unhelpful all evening, making what should have been an enjoyable family occasion a stressful and unpleasant one.

In summary, I am extremely disappointed by the service we received on Friday. Unless I receive some assurances that service standards have improved, I will not be dining at Lexington's again.

Students' opinions will vary on whether the letter will get a response. However, the writer has managed to make his opinion clear without getting overly emotional. In addition, he has made it clear that he is a regular customer who is normally very happy with the restaurant. A good restaurant manager would be likely to respond to such a letter with an apology and perhaps an offer such as a free meal to encourage the customer to return.

2   1 c   2 e   3 a   4 b   5 d   6 f

3 Sample answers:

1 Until recently, the service I have received from telephone banking has been excellent. However, recently I have been very disappointed by the service you have provided.
2 I was extremely disappointed to discover that the bicycle I purchased from your shop has several badly-damaged parts.
3 Unless I receive an apology for the insulting behaviour of your shop assistant, I will not be shopping with you again.

Language focus

1

… were told by a very rude waitress to wait at the bar until our table was ready.

… the waitress said she was too busy and we would have to wait.

Christopher is using reported speech to show what the waitress said.

2

1 He said there was nothing wrong with my washing machine.
2 She told me she couldn't help me with my problem.
3 He said he was too busy to serve me and that I'd have to wait.
4 She promised she would get someone to call me back soon.

Get writing

1 Sample answers:

1 Your customer service representative told me he would call back, but he did not.
2 The sandwich I ate at your restaurant gave me food poisoning. I am very concerned about the standards in your kitchen, and worried that other customers may experience the same problems.
3 I am very disappointed that you have not yet refunded the money you owe me. Unfortunately, unless this matter is resolved within 30 days, I will have to seek legal advice.

2 Sample answer:

[Your address]
[Date]

Credit Card Services
Flex Bank
PO Box 1234
London SW1 9AE

Dear sir/madam,

Flex Credit Card Account Number 12345678: Failure to refund overpayment

I am writing to complain about the fact that you have failed to return my money to me.

On February 14 2011 I phoned your Customer Services Department to close my credit card account and made a final payment of £165. Your representative closed my account and wrote to me confirming that this had been done.

When I received the letter and final statement on 20 February, I saw that I had overpaid my account by £85 (I had recently returned a coat whose cost had also been paid to my card). I phoned your Customer Services Department immediately. The person I spoke to told me that there would be no problem with getting my money back. She said that a payment would be made to my bank account to refund my overpayment.

It is now May and I still have not received my money. I have called your company repeatedly, without results. While I agree with your adviser who said that the overpayment was 'my mistake' (phone call 14 April 2012), I do not think that it is acceptable to keep money that is actually mine.

Until recently I have been impressed with the customer service at your company. However, I am extremely disappointed with the way you have handled this situation. Unless I hear from you within 30 days I will ask for legal advice on how to recover the money you owe me.

Yours faithfully,

Francesca Schulmann

Unit 15 Applying for a job: your CV

Writing clearly

1 1 Personal Statement 2 Education/Qualifications 3 Work Experience 4 Skills 5 Referees

2 experienced, reliable, hardworking, polite, fluent, confident, good

Looking more closely

Model answers:

2 I worked in a busy office for two years.

3 I stay late and always do more than my boss expects.
4 I am well presented, polite and always do exactly what I am asked to do.
5 I can use lots of different software packages and have used computers confidently for many years.

Language focus

1 2 Answered 3 Wrote, did 4 Drove 5 Served 6 Prepared 7 Packed 8 Delivered 9 Taught 10 Translated

2

2   Serving customers, keeping the café clean and tidy, helping in the kitchen.
3   Serving customers, working on the till, keeping the shelves well stocked.
4   Keeping the house/office clean and tidy, vacuuming and dusting, cleaning windows.
5   Supervising staff, keeping a staff rota, dealing with customer queries and staff training.

Get writing

1   Example personal statement:

I am a hardworking and professional engineering graduate with experience in a variety of engineering-related areas including health and safety and construction. I am looking for a challenging role where I can combine my academic and practical skills as an engineer.

2   Example CV (including an Achievements section):

Steven Parker
49 Andover Street, Newcastle, N6 9QS
078863432331
steven.parker33@email.co.uk

Personal statement
I am an organized, confident and hardworking office manager with five years' experience. I am a polite

---

and professional communicator and enjoy working directly with the public. I always work hard to meet my goals and try to be much more than just 'good enough'. I am currently looking to move forward in my career with a more challenging role.

Achievements

*   Promoted to the role of General Office Manager at Johnston's Sports Centre.
*   Won a national award for bravery after rescuing stranded hillwalkers during Mountain Guide training.
*   Completed the Newcastle half marathon, raising £2,000 for charity.

Experience
Johnston's Sports Centre General Office Manager
2008–Present

*   Providing administrative support to the Sports Centre team.
*   Maintaining a new filing system.
*   Answering queries from customers.
*   Hiring and training new staff.

Newcastle City Housing Department Office Junior
2006–2008

*   Provided administrative support to manager of busy department.
*   Did filing and other general office duties.

Unit 16   Applying for a job: your covering letter

Understanding

This covering letter is an email. The name of the job and the candidate's name are included in the subject line. The letter is addressed to 'Mr Gregory'. The first line states the purpose of the letter, re-states which job is being applied for and says where Madeleine saw it advertised (this is useful if the company is recruiting for several jobs at the same time).

The first paragraph summarizes Madeleine's experience and mentions some of her skills and the award she won in her current job. She also explains why she wants to move to a new job.

The second paragraph explains why she is a suitable candidate for the role at Dragonflies. She mentions that her CV is attached.

She finishes by saying 'I very much look forward to hearing from you' – a standard finishing line for a covering letter – and signs off with her full name.

Looking more closely

1   She saw the job advertised in *The List* on 1st March.
2   5 years' experience in the bar industry (currently an Assistant Bar Manager); experience of hiring, training and managing staff, as well as creating cocktails.
3   Madeleine helped to win an award for her current employer by creating innovative cocktail recipes.
4   She feels that her wide-ranging experience, enthusiasm and drive can help her to make Dragonflies a more profitable business.

Writing appropriately

Sample answers:

✗   exam grades – Unless you are a school leaver, or the employer specifically asks you to include your exam grades, this is probably too much information for a covering letter.
✓   work experience – Many employers skim read CVs, so a quick summary of your most relevant work experience is a good thing to put in a covering letter.
(✓)   your address – If you were applying for a job by email, you would not need to add your address to the email. However, if you were applying by post, your covering letter should include your full address. Regardless of how you apply, your address should always appear in your CV.
✗   your age – In many English-speaking countries it is actually illegal for employers to ask you about your age, and it is not necessary to include it (or your date of birth) in a job application.
✓   why you want to leave – Yes, but be cautious about what you say. It is better to focus on the positives (e.g. you are looking for a more challenging role, you are moving to a new city, or you want a job to match your particular skills) than to mention negative reasons for seeking a new job.
(✗)   present salary – It is normally best to wait until the interview stage to discuss financial matters. However, some employers will ask you to give

your expected salary or day rate in your covering letter, in which case you should do so.

Language focus

1

I am applying for the post of Full-time Bar Manager, as advertised in *The List* on Friday 1 March.

I am an experienced and versatile bar person, <u>having worked</u> in the industry for the past five years in a number of increasingly responsible roles. I am currently Assistant Bar Manager at the bar-restaurant Olive, where I <u>not only</u> helped hire, train and manage a team of enthusiastic young bar people, <u>but</u> created a popular cocktails list to complement our food menu. <u>As a direct result</u>, Olive recently won an award for its cocktail innovation. I have really enjoyed working in such a demanding and rewarding role; <u>nevertheless</u> I feel that I am more than ready to meet the challenge of running a city-centre bar single-handed.

<u>Because of</u> my experience and drive, and <u>since</u> I have worked in a wide range of bar-restaurants, I believe that I have what it takes to successfully manage Dragonflies Bar-Restaurant and develop it into an even more profitable business. I would welcome the opportunity to prove my knowledge and ability in such an exciting new environment. <u>Therefore</u>, I would be very grateful if you would consider my application. My CV is attached, in pdf format as requested.

2

1 Because *OR* As a result   2 Not only
3 Due to the fact   4 because
5 Consequently *OR* As a result

Get writing

Sample answer:

> [Your address]
> [Date]
>
> Ms M Thornton
> Deskworld plc
> Langans Road
> Eastleigh SO53 2AJ
>
> Dear Ms Thornton,
>
> Please find enclosed my Curriculum Vitae in application to the post of Administrative Assistant at Deskworld plc.
>
> As you will see from my CV, I have four years' experience of working in office administration in a number of different environments. I have provided administrative support both to individuals and to larger teams with equal success. Consequently, I have learned to work very flexibly, and am able to learn new processes very quickly.
>
> In my previous roles I have developed strong organizational skills, attention to detail and an ability to work with speed and accuracy. I feel that these are key attributes for a successful administrator, and I would welcome the chance to demonstrate them, and to learn even more, within the offices of Deskworld plc.
>
> I bring commitment, energy, and excellent communication skills to the office every day, and therefore feel that that I could be a valuable addition to your team at Deskworld.
>
> I would greatly appreciate it if you would consider my application.
>
> Sincerely,
>
> Ruben Montero

Unit 17   Travel blogging

Understanding

The blog is about a round-the-world trip. The trip starts in the United States, and the writer and her travelling companion then go to Quito in Ecuador, and from there into the mountains to a place called Casa Mojanda. After a couple of days they go to the market in a town called Otavalo.

Writing appropriately

1

… the winding mountain roads ….

The view out of every window in the house is spectacular: volcanos, rolling green hills, farmland, grazing cows and horses, and gorgeous plants and trees.

Even the buildings here are beautiful.

… we are surrounded by cottages, a dining room, a library, and a wood-fired hot tub outdoors with a view of the volcano Nevado Cotacachi.

3

The author uses adjectives like 'spectacular' and 'amazing' to show that the first sight of the Amazon river was particularly special. In addition, the author says 'nothing had prepared me for my first sight of the Amazon', 'I've never seen anything like it.' and 'I will remember it forever'.

Language focus

1

The flight was spectacular. (past simple) The author uses the past simple here to talk about a completed action in the past. The flight was spectacular while it was happening, but it has finished now.

I've never seen anything like it … (present perfect) The author uses the present perfect here to talk about something that began in the past and is still relevant now. Nothing the author has seen in the past is as amazing as that first sight of the Amazon, and that is still true when the blog post is being written.

2

Answers will vary, but they should use the present perfect tense:

1   The most amazing thing I've ever seen is …
2   The most memorable journey I've ever taken is …
3   The craziest place I've ever visited is …

Get writing

7   Sample answer:

> **Landing in Lima, Peru**
> **October 1 2012 by Wanderguy**
>
> I've been to some crazy cities before, but Lima must surely be the craziest! We finally landed in Lima at 10pm yesterday evening after nearly 24 hours of exhausting travel. We were met at the airport by our bad-tempered taxi driver who loaded our bags without a word and drove us to the hotel. Lima traffic is terrifying! Every driver changes lane without warning, shouts out of their window, honks their horn and shakes their fist at passing drivers, with their radios blaring all the time. We were so relieved to arrive at the hotel, drink one cold coke, and get to bed.
>
> **I love Iquitos!**
>
> October 3 2012 **by Wanderguy**
>
> We've just enjoyed our first full day in the marvellous city of Iquitos. We'd been worried about what we were

getting into when we arrived at its airport yesterday morning. The airport is simply one long wooden hall at the side of a muddy runway. A German Shepherd dog sniffed briefly at our luggage and that, I believe, is what passes for 'airport security' here. However, our taxi driver was friendly, helpful, and spoke English fluently. This made us feel better about the bullet hole in the windscreen of his car. He left us at our hotel in Iquitos and within minutes we were exploring! What a fantastic city this is. Beautiful buildings, fabulous food, music, friendly people and a real 'fiesta' feel.

Meeting the Amazon River

October 6 2012 **by Wanderguy**

This morning, we said a fond goodbye to the stunning city of Iquitos and said hello to the Amazon River. We took a crazy 'motocarro' (a rickshaw fixed onto the back of a moped) from our little hotel to the Port of Iquitos and saw our boat for the very first time. We watched incredibly strong local men load our luggage, provisions, and equipment onto the boat, as well as our food for the trip. This included a few chickens, one pig, and a goat! We were shown our tiny but immaculate cabin, then stood on the deck as we left Iquitos behind. As I write this, and after watching the city of Iquitos fade into the distance, we are heading into the heart of the Amazon and two weeks of adventure.

Unit 18   Tweeting

Understanding

The example tweets have a number of purposes:

1   @GlasgowProjectManager is looking for someone with particular experience to work on a project, so he is asking people who follow him to recommend people to him.
2   @CaroMarathonWoman is sharing information about her preparations for a marathon run. Perhaps she is looking for other people doing similar things, or maybe she is just updating her followers.
3   @Manchester_Music_Fan is asking for advice on his next phone purchase. Twitter is a popular place for sharing information on new technology products and services.
4   @Josephine_Gourmet is updating her followers on a restaurant she is visiting with another Twitter user. These types of tweets are for updating friends and for advertising local places that other Twitter users might want to try.
5   @MsGeniusWebDev is a web developer who is looking for work. She has seen @GlasgowProjectManager's tweet and is replying to it. Twitter makes it easy to find people and information that might otherwise be hard to find (e.g. a Google search is not so helpful for finding people quickly for jobs).

Writing appropriately

1

1 timeline   2 @replies   3 DM   4 RT   5 hashtag

Language note: Hashtags are a useful way to share information on a topic that lots of people are interested in. For example, if lots of tweeters are at a conference, there will usually be a hashtag for that conference. Putting the hashtag after your tweets tells readers that you are tweeting about the conference, and allows other conference attendees to search and look at what you are saying.

Tweeters also use hashtags to draw attention to ideas or concepts. For example, in @Josephine_Gourmet's tweet, she uses the hashtag #spicy to draw attention to how spicy her pizza is. Hashtags are a new way of bringing attention to something – rather like a 21st century exclamation mark.

2

Sample answers:
(Remember not to go above 140 characters!)

1   @Manchester_Music_Fan I think you should wait a few months and then upgrade – you might save some money.

2   RT @Josephine_Gourmet Finally trying out @
    cornerpizzapalace. Enjoying a Pepperoni
    Extravaganza with @angelinanotsojolly. #spicy
3   I love Rihanna's new song! #Rihannarocks

Looking more closely

1

1 #CNNweather   2 #ISS   3 #endschoolbullying
4 #anti-ageing   5 #newspapers

2   Sample answer:

RT @Star_Sky_Gazer If in UK, look up tonight to
see a fantastically bright #ISS pass at 23.32, from
west to east. [Will be looking carefully. Hope it isn't
cloudy!]

3   Sample answer:

@Its_Good_to_Talk How many signatures does the
petition have so far? Hope it makes a real difference!

4   Sample answer:

@CassTravellingGirl Green tea supposed to be very good
for you, but I prefer my tea with milk! Let us know how
you get on.

Get writing

Answers will vary.

Unit 19   Reviewing online

Understanding

Answers will vary, but overall the review is good, and
makes the hotel seem appealing. Before making a decision,
it would be worth looking at a sample of other reviews to
see if other guests have the same high opinion of the hotel.

Looking more closely

1

1   someone else has told you they think it is good
2   someone has done something for you in an
    exemplary way. An example would be a waiter who
    was very attentive during a meal, answered all your
    questions, sorted out any problems and helped you
    to enjoy your meal.
3   you are happy with the price you paid and feel that
    you paid too little or just the right amount, rather
    than too much
4   at first you weren't happy with something. 'Initially'
    means 'at first', so this suggests that the situation
    improved later on.
5   in a good place. An 'ideally located hotel' is one that
    is close to the things you want to visit or see.
6   when someone takes care of your needs themselves.
    For example, if someone carries your bags to your
    hotel room, that is personal service.

2

1   Both. More commonly used to describe a service (e.g.
    the stylist was extremely professional), but could also
    describe a product (e.g. professional hair care products).
2   Service
3   Both. Usually describes a product (e.g. made of high-
    quality leather) but could also describe a service (e.g.
    Her teaching skills were of a high quality.)
4   Both
5   Product (e.g. The wooden toys were very well made.)
6   Both
7   Product (e.g. The model cars were poorly
    constructed and soon fell apart.)
8   Product (e.g. The alarm clock was damaged when it
    arrived in the post.)
9   Product (e.g. The Moroccan lamp fittings were
    beautifully crafted.)
10 Both (e.g. The staff handled the problem in an
    exemplary fashion./The quality of the diamond was
    exemplary.)

Language focus

The review is about a pair of hiking boots (specialist
boots used by people who like long walks outdoors in
difficult terrain). The review is unfavourable. The author
was disappointed by the fit and quality of the boots.

Writing appropriately

The review simply tells us that the author doesn't like
the Crazy Crayfish Cantina. We don't know if the
problem was with the food, the service, the décor, or
something else. A good review helps readers to make
an informed judgment about what is being reviewed
by giving specific examples of what went wrong, rather
than just an expression of their feelings about it.

Get writing

1   Sample answers:

1   'Useful and great value for money.'
2   'Wonderful gym – shame about the staff.'
3   'Damaged goods AND poor service = double trouble!'

2   Sample answer:

Online book review

The Man Who Saw Red (Darwin Books)

By Mortimer Dahl

'A fascinating introduction to how the brain works'
4 April 2012

A review by Harald Neumann (Germany)

This is an amazing insight into what happens when
the human brain goes wrong. I am not sure who
this book is actually written for, but that may be one
of its best features. While it will definitely appeal to
medical students, its personal observations will also

fascinate ordinary people like me who want to know how the brain works, and what happens if things go wrong. I hadn't been aware how fragile the brain is until I started reading this very moving book.

The author is an experienced neurologist, but still writes in a very clear way, avoiding jargon while

explaining complicated problems with compassion. He focuses on how his patients' lives are affected by their problems, rather than just making a diagnosis. I would recommend it to anyone with an interest in how the human mind works.

Unit 20   Selling and advertising online

Understanding

A three-piece suite is being sold. This is a set of living room furniture – usually a sofa and two armchairs made of the same materials. It seems like it may be a bargain. Although it is only six months old it still looks relatively new (only a few small marks) and the price has fallen from £1,100 to £550. However, something is only a bargain if (a) the buyer really wants/needs it and (b) the advert is honest about what is being sold.

Looking more closely

1   almost as good as when it was bought – no damage or defects beyond very minor marks or wear
2   a suitable size for three people to sit on
3   looking similar to the other items in the furniture set
4   treated gently and with care to avoid damage
5   with very little visible damage – maybe a few small marks that are hard to see.
6   the seller does not really want to sell the item; perhaps they are only doing so because they are moving house, for example.

Language focus

1

1   excellent condition
2   good working order
3   original packaging
4   good as new
5   immaculate condition

2   Sample answers:

1   The phone is as good as new.
2   Laptop is sold in its original packaging.
3   The bike is in good working order.
4   The sofa is good value for money.

Writing appropriately

1

1 c   2 a   3 e   4 b   5 d

2

The writers are looking for a responsible and friendly flatmate, who can be male or female but must not smoke or own a pet. Ideally they should be over 25, single and professional (working).

3

1   a flat or house that is rented with furniture in all the rooms
2   a person who does not smoke
3   a house that looks beautiful inside
4   a bed that can fit two people
5   a place for storing clothes that has been built into the room (i.e. it is not a separate piece of furniture)
6   close enough to walk to (i.e. you don't have to drive or take public transport to get there)

Get writing

1   Sample answers:

1   Highly experienced Spanish teacher offering lessons now.
2   Brilliant value games console – good as new with lots of extras.
3   Well-loved sofa needs a nice new home – going cheap!

2   Sample answers:

Wii Console, Wii fit board and games bundle BNIB

Wii Fit console and games for sale – brand new in all original packaging. All items unused – unwanted Christmas presents. In immaculate condition and perfect working order. Good as new.

- 1 x Wii console – boxed
- 2 x Wii remotes with grips
- 1 x Wii fit board – boxed
- Sensor bar and all leads included
- User manuals included

All items will be shipped together once payment is received – free collection if preferred, from SW19 Colliers Wood area.

Paypal or cash accepted.

Thanks for looking and happy bidding.

Mountfield SP 470 petrol lawnmower for sale.

Two years old, but in very good working order. Recently serviced and carefully maintained. There are signs of acceptable cosmetic wear – paint scratches, scrapes etc., however all workings are fully operational.

Sold as seen.

£9.99 P&P or free pick-up.

Collins
English for Life

Would you also like to listen, read and speak fluently?

- Authentic: real English prepares you for the language you will come across in life
- Practical: learn strategies to understand and to produce natural English
- Comprehensive: learn and gain confidence with a broad variety of accents, texts and contexts

Collins English for Life: Listening

978-0-00-745872-1

🎵 Includes audio CD

Collins English for Life: Reading

978-0-00-745871-4

Collins English for Life: Speaking

978-0-00-745783-0

🎵 Includes audio CD

Also available from Collins

CEF Level: B2

Agatha Christie English Readers

Collins English Readers help you get the most out of Agatha Christie's crime stories.

- Language suitable for language learners
- Notes on history and culture
- Character notes
- Glossary of difficult words
- Audio CD with reading of the story

Available internationally from all good bookshops. If you need help finding your local stockist, please email us, telling us where you live, at collins.elt@harpercollins.co.uk.

www.collinselt.com